Hamp

a drama
John Wilson

based on an episode from the novel
Return to the Wood by J. L. Hodson

SAMUELFRENCH.COM
SAMUELFRENCH-LONDON.CO.UK

ISBN 978 0 573 04018 4

INTRODUCTION

This story is about a group of men who, required to implement a law they believe to be in principle necessary and just, experience its workings in practice as horrifyingly wrong.

It is the law which defines their Army's right to punish desertion by death. They believe that the circumstances of their war, in particular the possibility of mass desertions from their Army, justify its assumption of this right. Yet they find that the death of their own deserter, Hamp, even while they are preparing for it in the ceremony of a court-martial, is unimaginable to them. It is quite unthinkable—yet it must happen. When it does happen, they know they are taking part in an act of ritual murder.

They know that in terms of their law Hamp has been justly proved guilty beyond any doubt; but for the rest of their lives they will not be able to forget his innocence.

JOHN WILSON

PRODUCTION NOTE

As Webb says, Hamp is gormless. He is a pathetic figure, to everyone but himself. If Hamp knows anything at all, it is that he is unimportant. It is this which explains his gratitude that an officer should be taking the trouble to defend him, and his certainty that everything will be all right because they all have more urgent things to attend to than shooting him. In any case, he is incapable of speculation on his fate, so he does not feel real fear or self-pity—not until his fate is finally known.

In one respect, Hamp is right; the officers really are too busy with the war to bother with his wholly understandable crime. But whereas Hamp comforts himself with the belief that his betters are in charge of the situation, they know that they are not. Each in his own way finds the whole business tiresome and worrying. Hargreaves' approach at first is detached; he wants to do his necessary but unpleasant duty and get it over. But Hamp's total lack of comprehension and blind faith involve him in spite of himself. Webb is impatient of the whole time-wasting paraphernalia of *ad hoc* law administration. He has sympathy for Hamp—for all the unhappy protagonists of this wretched affair—but he keeps it hidden, exaggerating his own cynicism in an attempt to shield himself and the others from the horror of what they are doing. The Medical Officer, O'Sullivan, is a very weary man—a man who has done and is doing his duty doggedly and unstintingly, and for whom it must be a bitter experience to be called to account for a trifling failure of understanding several months earlier.

One set can be used for both the barn and the court-martial scene. The photographs show the design used at Edinburgh, which gave a feeling of space and erstwhile splendour, now reduced to dilapidation. The shutter effect also helped to remind the audience that this was Belgium.

If spreading straw around creates difficulties, a rampart of straw bales can be used. Then Hamp can remain behind the bales, out of sight, until Hargreaves enters and Hamp has to stand up.

The oath administered in the court-martial is as follows: 'I swear by Almighty God that the evidence I shall give to this court-martial shall be the truth, the whole truth and nothing but the truth', and is taken on the Bible, as in a court of law.

HAMP

The first performance of this play took place at the Theatre Royal, Newcastle, on 11th August, 1964. It was subsequently produced at the Lyceum Theatre, Edinburgh, with the following cast:

PRIVATE ARTHUR HAMP	*John Hurt*
CORPORAL OF GUARD	*Malcolm Tierney*
GUARD PRIVATE	*Jon Croft*
LIEUTENANT WILLIAM HARGREAVES	*Richard Briers*
LIEUTENANT TOM WEBB	*Leonard Rossiter*
PRESIDENT OF THE COURT	*Noel Coleman*
MEMBERS OF THE COURT	*Christopher Greatorex*
	Jeremy Conway
LIEUTENANT PRESCOTT	*Michael Deacon*
PROSECUTING OFFICER (MIDGLEY)	*Charles Hodgson*
PADRE	*Tom Watson*
M. O. (O'SULLIVAN)	*Kevin Flood*
ORDERLY OFFICER	*Jeremy Conway*

The play was directed by JOHN GIBSON
with décor by CHRISTOPHER MORLEY

The action of the play takes place on the Western Front in 1917 during the Battle of Passchendaele.

ACT ONE	The army prison.
ACT TWO	The Court Martial room. One week later.
ACT THREE	
SCENE 1	Army prison. Two weeks later.
SCENE 2	The same. Next morning.

No character in this play is intended to portray any specific person, alive or dead.

ACT I

Near Passchendaele. 1917.
Scene includes interior of small barn, part of outside wall of barn with door, and section of farmyard outside.
Intermittent gunfire is heard.
Inside the barn HAMP is behind a bale of straw, not seen by the audience. A CORPORAL sits writing a report. Mouth organ music is heard from HAMP.

CORPORAL You'll get me in trouble, you know.
          (Music stops. HAMP looks over straw.)
HAMP   Eh?
CORPORAL Should've taken that away from you by rights. Better keep it a bit quiet.
HAMP   Hey, Corp, what d'you reckon they'll do wi' me, like?
CORPORAL Not for the likes of me to reckon anything on it.
HAMP   Expect it'll come out all right, eh?
CORPORAL (a little sharply, because he is anxious to get the message over) Listen, lad, you can't hardly expect—I mean you can't reckon on—getting off. Not right off. You've got to reckon on them doing something about it, haven't you?
GUARD   (off) Corporal!
          (GUARD PRIVATE and LIEUTENANT HARGREAVES enter farmyard and approach door. CORPORAL gets up hurriedly and goes to door, opening it as they approach, meeting them just outside it and closing it behind him. CORPORAL salutes and HARGREAVES returns salute.)
HARGREAVES Stand easy, Corporal. Your prisoner's here, is he?
CORPORAL Yes, sir.

(*Meanwhile,* HAMP—*still, of course, inside the barn—pockets his mouth-organ, rises, and stands listening near the door.*)

HARGREAVES　How is he behaving?

CORPORAL　He's—oh yes, he's all right, sir.

HARGREAVES　No trouble?

CORPORAL　No, sir.

GUARD　He's not like that, sir.

CORPORAL　Only, he doesn't know how it could turn out. He doesn't give no sign of knowing, sir, if you see what I mean.

GUARD　That's true, sir. You can't help remarkin' on it. It's like he's not much bothered most of the time.

(HAMP, *meanwhile, has lost interest and is now going around looking for eggs among the straw. He finds two or three and puts them in his cap.*)

CORPORAL　To let you understand, sir—he's bound to know, like, the way it could turn out, but—you'll see for yourself, sir—he doesn't believe it.

HARGREAVES　You've spoken to him about it, then?

CORPORAL　Not really, sir, but——

HARGREAVES　But you've let him speak to you about it?

CORPORAL　Well, yes, sir, a bit. I know it's laid down we shouldn't, but——

GUARD　You can't 'ardly help it, sir—a bit, like. Specially with one like him.

CORPORAL　Perhaps when you see him, sir, you——

HARGREAVES　When procedures and duties are laid down there's usually a good reason for them.

CORPORAL　Yes, sir.

HARGREAVES　And even if you don't fully understand the reason you're still required to carry out the duties as laid down—will you remember that?

CORPORAL　Yes, sir.

(HARGREAVES *moves to open door into barn.*)

Shall I come in with you, sir?

HARGREAVES　No. I'll talk to him alone. Stand by in the Guard Room. I'll call you before I leave.

CORPORAL　(*saluting*) Sir.

(HARGREAVES *returns salute, opens door and goes into barn.*)

HAMP Who were that, Corp?

(*Exeunt* CORPORAL *and* GUARD. *During all this time* HAMP *has been searching for nesting places in the straw. This has gone on until the door is actually opened, and he is therefore, when* HARGREAVES *first sees him, even less tidy-looking than usual, with traces of straw sticking to his tunic and trousers.*)

HARGREAVES Private Hamp.

HAMP (*trying a soldierly salute*) Sir.

HARGREAVES Lieutenant Hargreaves.

HAMP Yes, sir. I know you, sir.

HARGREAVES Do you? How?

HAMP Time of Trones Wood, sir. Arras as well—and other times.

HARGREAVES How long have you been out here?

HAMP '14, sir. Coming on three year.

HARGREAVES You know that you're entitled to the help of a Defending Officer at your court martial?

HAMP Yes, sir. Soldier's Friend.

HARGREAVES Subject to your acceptance, at the request of your Platoon Commander, I've agreed to represent you. It so happens I'm a solicitor by profession—a lawyer—so I can probably be as much help to you as anybody. Subject, as I say, to your acceptance.

HAMP Yes, sir.

HARGREAVES You've no objection, then?

HAMP Oh no, sir. I have to thank you, sir. I mean, it's not same as you have to do it.

HARGREAVES Someone has to.

HAMP But I mean, it's very good of you, isn't it?

HARGREAVES Anyhow, if we've settled that—before we go any further, Hamp, I don't know why you've been allowed to get into the disgracefully unsoldierlike condition you're in now, but understand this, man—I will not put up with it so long as I have anything to do with you.

HAMP I never knew it mattered, like, sir—I mean in here.

HARGREAVES I'm telling you now it does matter.

HAMP   Yes, sir.
HARGREAVES Slackness and sloppiness always matter.
HAMP   Yes, sir.
HARGREAVES Stand easy. Now remember what I've told you. I shouldn't have *had* to tell you, as a matter of simple discipline, but apart from that it's for your own good.
HAMP   Yes, sir.
HARGREAVES If I'm going to help you I expect you to do all you can to help yourself, maintain your own standards.
HAMP   Yes, sir.
HARGREAVES (*taking note-book and pencil from his pocket*) Now, I require to take some notes about your case. Sit down, will you?
            (*They both sit down.* HARGREAVES *opens note-book and reads from it.*)
            Eight-seven-three-four-two-six.
HAMP   Yes, sir.
HARGREAVES Age?
HAMP   Twenty-three, sir.
HARGREAVES Occupation?
HAMP   Well, I suppose it's soldiering, sir. Least up till this lot.
HARGREAVES But you weren't a regular soldier, were you?
HAMP   Oh no, sir. Only from '14.
HARGREAVES I mean your occupation in civilian life.
HAMP   Same as you nearly forget, like, sir, isn't it?
HARGREAVES What was it?
HAMP   I had a trade, sir. I were what they call a Little Piecer. It's a trade in t'mills. Cotton, like.
HARGREAVES Yes—I've heard of it.
HAMP   Lamton I come from.
HARGREAVES Yes, I have a note of that. Now——
HAMP   D'you know it, like, sir?
HARGREAVES Mm?
HAMP   Lamton. I were wondering if you——
HARGREAVES Yes, I do know it as a matter of fact. My home's not far from there.
HAMP   I were just wondering.
HARGREAVES Had you always worked in the mill?
HAMP   Well, like, since I left t'school, sir.

HARGREAVES When was that?

HAMP Long while now, sir.

HARGREAVES Yes, but I mean, how old were you?

HAMP Twelve, sir.

HARGREAVES And this was your only job from then until the time when you joined up?

HAMP Weren't much else in Lamton, sir, were there? You would know. Same as—— (*Pause.*)

HARGREAVES Yes?

HAMP No—I were only going to say, same as my father and grandad afore. My grandad did sixteen hours a day in his time.

HARGREAVES Yes. I——

HAMP 'Course, I never knew him—not proper. He passed away, like, when I were only little.

HARGREAVES Are you married?

HAMP Yes, sir.

(HARGREAVES *expects more, but this subject stops the talkative flow.*)

HARGREAVES Any children?

HAMP Yes, sir.

HARGREAVES How many?

HAMP One, sir. A little lad.

HARGREAVES You understand why I have to ask these questions?

HAMP Well, you know best, sir.

HARGREAVES It will help me if I know something about the circumstances of your home life.

HAMP Does that come into it then, sir?

HARGREAVES It may, in one way or another. Are you—are you on good terms with your wife?

HAMP Speaking of home life, you see, sir, we hadn't really got a place. Always lived with her mother, like.

HARGREAVES You see, what I want to know is—has there been something worrying you, something preying on your mind —about your home life? I know that such a thing can very seriously affect any soldier's morale. Am I right in thinking that, apart from any question of housing difficulties—that you're not on very good terms with your wife?

HAMP Did somebody say summat to you then, sir?

HARGREAVES Well, your Platoon Commander mentioned that he'd wondered about it, that was all.

HAMP Lieutenant Webb. He's a good man, sir.

HARGREAVES Don't you want to answer my question?

HAMP About t'wife?

HARGREAVES Yes.

HAMP Oh. She's took up with somebody else, sir—so I were told.

HARGREAVES Who told you?

HAMP I got a letter.

HARGREAVES From whom?

HAMP Charlie Scudder in Lamton. I know the other chap as well.

HARGREAVES And this has been worrying you? Preying on your mind?

HAMP I weren't surprised.

HARGREAVES No, perhaps not, but——

HAMP She hadn't much sense, sir. Needed looking after.

HARGREAVES But surely, man, you—Well, in any case it must have affected your judgment—your discipline. That's understandable. And, you see, it's important for your defence. This must have had some connection with what you did. It's important for us to establish mitigating circumstances. This is something anyone can understand. Any court will understand it and sympathise with it.

HAMP You mean like an excuse, sir?

HARGREAVES Well, a reason—an understandable reason.

HAMP I reckon you know best, sir.

HARGREAVES Did you keep that letter?

HAMP Charlie's letter?

HARGREAVES The one about your wife.

HAMP No, sir. I never thought.

HARGREAVES Still, you must have mentioned it to someone at the time—told your friends something about it? Didn't you?

HAMP Yes, I did that, sir. Willie Bryson. Private Bryson in our Platoon. Only——

HARGREAVES He would remember if we asked him, surely?

HAMP I thought you would maybe know him, sir.

HARGREAVES Bryson? No, I don't think so. Why?

HAMP He got killed, sir.

HARGREAVES Wasn't there anyone else you talked to about this?

HAMP Like, Willie, sir—he were from along our street.

HARGREAVES You mean you told him because he would have heard about it in any case, in his own letters?

HAMP Turned out he were told before me.

HARGREAVES (the lawyer taking over) And you didn't share the worry with anyone else? Apart from telling—(Consulting notes.) Bryson about it—and of course you knew that he would learn from other sources—apart from that you decided to suffer the anxiety of it within your own mind. For better or worse, you chose to keep it bottled up inside yourself, in your own private thoughts, and of course——

HAMP Is that what I've to say, like, sir? Is that what you want me to say?

HARGREAVES (stopped short) Now look here, man. Make no mistake about this. I do not want you now or at any time to say anything that isn't the truth, is that understood?

HAMP Yes, sir.

HARGREAVES Well, then—what is the truth about this? Did this trouble and anxiety about your wife have any bearing on what you did?

HAMP I don't know, sir.

HARGREAVES You what?

HAMP Well, you said particular I were to tell you the truth, sir, and that's the truth—I couldn't rightly say. I never thought much on it. Like, you don't want to think much on the like of that. But if you say it were something to do with that——

HARGREAVES My God, man, don't you understand? That's for you to say, not me! But I—I do advise you to give some thought to it between now and the time of your trial. Think very carefully about it. We'll talk about it again.

HAMP Yes, sir. (Pause.) D'you think it'll come out all right, sir?

HARGREAVES   What d'you mean—all right? It can't be all right. Don't you realise, man, this is——

HAMP   What I mean is, sir—like, they could make this into a shooting job, according to rights. According to the book, like.

HARGREAVES   (*gravely*) So you are aware of that?

HAMP   But I expect it'll come out all right.

HARGREAVES   (*after a baffled pause*) Tell me, Hamp—why did you enlist?

HAMP   Same as everybody else I reckon, sir.

HARGREAVES   No, that won't do. Think back.

HAMP   (*trying it out, because he has to say something*) Well, king and country, sir.

HARGREAVES   That does you credit, if it's true.

HAMP   They egged me on as well.

HARGREAVES   You mean they dared you to join up?

HAMP   Aye, sir, it were more that than——

HARGREAVES   Who did?

HAMP   (*trying to be crafty*) Well, like, the wife, sir.

HARGREAVES   (*hopefully*) Is that true?

HAMP   Well, I could say it, if——

HARGREAVES   Now, Hamp, I warned you!

HAMP   She never said anything against it—and that's not telling a lie.

HARGREAVES   Did anyone—dare you?

HAMP   Well, it were her mother mostly. They never thought I would go, but I did.

HARGREAVES   But you must also have thought of your duty to serve —to do your best for your country.

HAMP   Oh aye. Course, it were something new as well. And a right surprise for a lot of them. The wife's mother, and most of them in the street. And, same as all the lads say as well, sir, we never knew what it were going to be like, did we?

HARGREAVES   No, that's true enough. But——

HAMP   Like, when you think about it, we never had no way of knowing—none of us. Same as I were thinking to myself, sir—up there—that up there— it's a sight worse than anything, isn't it? It's a sight worse than anything you could think on—before like.

HARGREAVES If you had known what it was going to be like, would you have stayed at home?

HAMP (*almost attempting a joke*) Better if I had, sir, way it's turned out now. Would've saved you a lot of bother for one.

HARGREAVES But battle conditions have been the same for everybody. No worse for you than anybody else.

HAMP No, sir. But it were only because you were asking me, like.

HARGREAVES Yes, all right.

HAMP What I did, sir—I know I shouldn't 'ave. But it was same as I couldn't 'elp it.

HARGREAVES (*referring to notes*) Yes, we'll come to that later. You must have been among the first to come out here?

HAMP That's right, sir. Kitchener's Army, like.

HARGREAVES How did that happen? I mean, it must have been very soon after you joined up.

HAMP Well, at t'Depot, sir, there was a lot of Reservists getting sent out, and they wanted some of our lot to fill up, so I said I'd be one.

HARGREAVES So you volunteered for that too. (*He has at last found something worth entering in the note-book.*)

HAMP Course, we didn't know no better.

HARGREAVES Now you'd better be careful. (*Although he wants to smile at this.*)

HAMP That were what the lads used to say. Just a manner of speakin', sir.

HARGREAVES We'll have to teach you to be much more careful of your manner of speaking, my lad. You're going to need all the sympathy you can get at the trial, and you'll get damned little with that kind of talk.

HAMP That lot I came out with—there's none of them left, only for me.

HARGREAVES Are you listening?

HAMP Yes, sir.

HARGREAVES Since you came out here where have you been?

HAMP Well, a lot of different places, sir.

HARGREAVES You mentioned Trones Wood and Arras. Where else?

HAMP   Loos, sir—that were the first. That were a long time, that one. An' Gommycore.

HARGREAVES   Have you been wounded?

HAMP   Not proper, sir. I were bleeding a few times. And there were one time I got sent down to a G.C.S., but it weren't anything much. They sent me back the next day.

HARGREAVES   You've been lucky.

HAMP   Yes, sir.

HARGREAVES   Or, I suppose, unlucky—according to the way you look at it.

HAMP   I've heard some of our lads wishing they could lose an arm or a leg. And, same as everybody else, sir, I've heard tell of some that've tried it on themselves.

HARGREAVES   Did you ever think of that?

HAMP   You can't help it, sir, and that's the truth. It comes into your head.

HARGREAVES   Have you ever tried it?

HAMP   No, sir. Me and Willie Bryson once, sir, we was thinking of trying it, like, but we never did.

HARGREAVES   You can forget about that.

HAMP   It weren't long after when Willie's number came up.

HARGREAVES   And nobody else knew?

HAMP   Like, about Willie and me, sir? Us thinking about—?

HARGREAVES   Yes.

HAMP   No, sir.

HARGREAVES   As I say, then, forget it. Unless you're particularly asked, and I'll try to make sure you won't be. Just keep off the subject.

HAMP   Yes, sir.

HARGREAVES   On the whole I think the less you say, except yes or no, the better.

HAMP   I'll do my best, sir. Like, I'll try not to let you down.

HARGREAVES   (*patiently*) It's not a question of letting me down. I mean for your own sake, man, not mine. It matters a damned sight more to you than it does to me, doesn't it?

HAMP   Yes, sir I expect it'll come out all right now, though, if you're going to speak for me. You can say it better.

HARGREAVES   The point is, what am I going to say? You haven't been much help to me so far, I can tell you that. What

I want to know now is, I want you to tell me, clearly, carefully, and in as much detail as you can remember, exactly how this happened. I know when and where it happened, but I want you to tell me in your own words how.

HAMP   Not much to tell, sir. It were just a matter of—it were just a matter of running away from it. There's no sense in saying any different, like, sir, for that's what I did— an' I got caught.

HARGREAVES   Did you expect not to get caught?

HAMP   I don't know, sir.

HARGREAVES   You must surely have thought about it? Surely you——
(*He breaks off because* HAMP *has moved over towards the door and is reaching for a short piece of rope or thick string which is hanging there, attached, through the wall of the barn, to a little bell outside.*)
What are you doing?
(HAMP *pulls the string and the bell tinkles.*)

HAMP   Beg pardon, sir, but——

HARGREAVES   What the hell are you doing, man?

HAMP   Well, I—I have to go someplace, sir. I'm sorry, sir. When they hear the bell they know, like.

HARGREAVES   Yes. All right.
(*The* CORPORAL *and the* GUARD *have come on and into the barn.*)

CORPORAL   (*saluting*) Sir. Is it——?

HARGREAVES   (*returning salute*) Escort to the latrine.

CORPORAL   Yes, sir. (*Nods to* GUARD.)

GUARD   Prisoner, Shun!
(HAMP *does.*)
Quick—march!
(*They march out of door and off.*)

HARGREAVES   Stand easy, Corporal.

CORPORAL   Is he——? Well, I'm sorry, sir. He might have waited. But you can't say no, sir, can you?

HARGREAVES   No, that's all right. In any case, this might take quite a long time yet.

CORPORAL   Yes, I daresay, sir. D'you think he——?

HARGREAVES   Yes?

B

CORPORAL I was only wonderin' what you make of it.

HARGREAVES Even if that were a proper question, Corporal, I couldn't tell you.

CORPORAL Shouldn't fancy your job, sir. He's got his own way of looking at things, as you might say.

HARGREAVES (rueful, not unfriendly) Yes. However, as you told me, he expects it'll be all right.

CORPORAL Lieutenant Webb's waiting for you in the Guard Room, sir.

HARGREAVES Yes, I did want to see him about this, but you'd better advise him not to wait. Lord knows when I'll be finished with—No, listen, Corporal, keep your prisoner in the Guard Room till I call for him, and in the meantime ask Lieutenant Webb if he'll come in here, will you?

CORPORAL Yes, sir.

(He goes out, leaving door open. HARGREAVES rolls and lights a cigarette. Enter WEBB.)

WEBB Hello Bill. Are you going to get this gormless little bastard off, d'you think?

HARGREAVES What's the matter with you?

WEBB All this bloody pomp and circumstance about—that.

HARGREAVES What would you do? Just shoot him?

WEBB It's going to happen anyway, isn't it?

HARGREAVES Not necessarily. In fact, not if I can help it.

WEBB By God, you mean it, don't you?

HARGREAVES You can't do this job without thinking a bit about it.

WEBB Dangerous game, Bill.

HARGREAVES Why the hell do they allow anything like that out here?

WEBB He's quite cheerful, I hear. Probably thinks his troubles are over now.

HARGREAVES What about his previous record? I thought he hadn't done too badly up till now. Told me you said so.

WEBB I suppose he tried. Anyhow, it doesn't count now.

HARGREAVES It might, if you're prepared to say it in court.

WEBB Take a damned sight more eloquence than I could manage before it would make any difference. Still, I'll do what you tell me.

HARGREAVES What have you got against him?

WEBB   He's a nuisance—a bloody nuisance. Waste of everybody's time. As if we hadn't enough to get on with.
(*Indicating direction of gunfire.*) All the blasted debate
there's going to be about—Still, I suppose there's no
way round it. Why don't you plead chronic softness in
the head?

HARGREAVES   Wish I could.

WEBB   Why not?

HARGREAVES   Because I don't think he is.

WEBB   He can do a very good imitation of it.

HARGREAVES   No, he wouldn't play up. That's what's so bloody baff-
ling about him. The only thing he's going to play up to
is the truth. He can't help it, but it's not going to help
me much. It's—funny thing is it's a kind of courage.
But it's damned awkward.

WEBB   Courage! By God, that's one word you'd better keep
out of your arguments in the court.

HARGREAVES   They couldn't really, in cold blood, shoot that, Tom,
could they?

WEBB   Wouldn't be the first time. You'd better try to keep
this professional, you know. Would it help if I stayed
when you're talking to him, by the way? I've a feeling
he's going to get a damned sight more sympathy from
you than he deserves—maybe more than's going to be
good for him.

HARGREAVES   No, Tom, this is my job.

WEBB   All right, I'll let you get on with it. We'll talk about it
later.

HARGREAVES   Yes, when I've finished with him I could do with your
help. For one thing, I want to find out a bit more about
what you've got against him. It's not like you. (*He has
moved towards the door, now calls out.*)
Corporal!

CORPORAL   (*as he comes on*) Sir.

HARGREAVES   Stand by to bring your prisoner in again, please.

CORPORAL   Yes, sir. (*Exit.*)

WEBB   There's one thing you're forgetting, Bill. All your talk
about 'will *they* shoot him?'—Private Gormless Gutless.
Well, *they* won't, will they? But, somebody's going to

get the job. I've been thinking about it too, you see, thinking about who's going to be O.C. Firing Squad— the instrument of justice as they say. Well, I've had a good look round, and, unless of course they found a volunteer——

HARGREAVES Not you, surely.

WEBB No? I reckon it's quite likely. They're always going on about being short of officers.

HARGREAVES But if you——

WEBB It's only a very small detail, of course, but—Anyhow, I'll do my best for him in Court. I've a very sound selfish reason for saying all you want me to say, and more.

HARGREAVES I'm not asking you to perjure yourself, you know. The truth'll do.

WEBB Too complicated for me, Bill, the truth about this one. It would take far too long, even if I wanted to think it out, which I don't.

HARGREAVES This firing squad thing, though. Surely if you asked— if you made a point of—they wouldn't compel you?

WEBB I wouldn't ask.

HARGREAVES Why not?

WEBB Because I'm here to do what I'm told.
(HAMP, CORPORAL *and* GUARD *re-enter, marching. Exit* WEBB.)

CORPORAL Prisoner! Halt!

HARGREAVES All right. Stand easy. Stand by again in the Guard Room, Corporal.

CORPORAL (*saluting*) Sir. (*He and* GUARD *go out.*)

HARGREAVES Now, Hamp, sit down. To get back to the point. I asked you—did you not *expect* to be arrested?

HAMP It's same as I never thought about it, sir, one way or t'other.

HARGREAVES Yes, all right. Leave that for the moment. But can you tell me *why* you desert—why you went absent?

HAMP I couldn't stand it no more, sir.

HARGREAVES But surely, man! I mean, why this time? After all you've been through——

HAMP It weren't the first time I thought about doing it, sir

HARGREAVES What?
      HAMP I nearly did it once afore, sir. I thought about it. It were
           time of Arras. I were sent back one time there on a
           water party. I were thinking about running away, but
           a Redcap got 'is eye on me, so I didn't.
HARGREAVES And that was all?
      HAMP Yes, sir.
HARGREAVES Forget about that too. Put it out of your mind.
      HAMP Yes, sir.
HARGREAVES But I want to know more about this time. Much more.
           I have to know. About how it happened and about the
           reasons and thoughts and motives that were in your
           mind.
      HAMP Same as I said, sir, I don't know no more to tell you.
           I couldn't stand it no more.
HARGREAVES But you're a soldier, man. You've got to stand it. You
           stood it all the other times.
      HAMP I'm not saying there were sense in it, sir, but——
HARGREAVES Suppose your comrades had ever run away and left *you*
           to it—say, at Loos, or Trones Wood—you'd have been
           in a fine mess, wouldn't you?
      HAMP (*after thinking about this*) I don't think it could've been
           much worse nor it were, sir—and that's the God's
           truth.
           (HARGREAVES *is momentarily silenced by this.*)
HARGREAVES All right. Now, from the beginning, tell me what
           happened.
      HAMP Well, I were in that attack, sir. It were very bad.
HARGREAVES Yes, I know.
      HAMP Didn't get wounded—but the time when this came into
           my head were—I got blown into a shell-hole. It were a
           deep one, deepest muck ever I saw. I thought I were
           done for, sure—getting sucked down into t'muck. Only
           just when I were going right under two of the lads saw
           it. They gave me butt-end of a rifle and they pulled me
           out. It's not sense, sir, but that were worse nor any-
           thing else that ever came on me afore. It were same as
           I couldn't get over it, like. I couldn't stand it no more
           —after.

HARGREAVES But you got out of it all right. And surely it was some
time after that attack when you—I mean, it wasn't a
case of running away in panic from the front line. After
that attack, as I understand it, your battalion was
relieved. You were sent back for a rest.

HAMP Yes, sir. A bit back.

HARGREAVES And it was from there, about ten days after the attack,
that you deserted.

HAMP Yes, sir.

HARGREAVES Why? Why then?

HAMP Same as I said, sir. I couldn't stand no more.

HARGREAVES You mean that from the time of the attack, and your
—from the time when you had that bad shock in the
shell-hole, you were in a continual state of fear. Is that
what you mean?

HAMP I think that's right, sir.

HARGREAVES *Is* that what you mean? Thinking is not good enough.
I've got to know. Was this something worse than the
normal feeling of fear before you went into action?

HAMP Honest, sir—it were worse, worse nor anything.

HARGREAVES (*after waiting for him to say more*) Yes? Please try to
tell me. This is what I want to know, in your own
words.

HAMP It were same as I—after the attack—after I got out o'
that shell-'ole—I were different, sir. Like—different in
myself.

HARGREAVES Yes? Tell me. In what way? This is important to you,
I promise you. In what way different?
(*There is a long, long, struggling pause—as much as ten
or twelve long seconds perhaps.*)

HAMP It were same as I said, sir. It's same as I can't say it no
different. I couldn't stand no more. I knew for sure I
couldn't stand no more. I can't say it no different.

HARGREAVES Even when you were out of the battle?

HAMP It were same as it didn't matter no more where, sir.
Any place I could hear guns.

HARGREAVES But God knows there's never a time when you can't
hear them somewhere!

HAMP That's right, sir.

HARGREAVES   Well, then, what——?
HAMP   I couldn't stand no more!
HARGREAVES   But——
HAMP   Lieutenant Webb, sir—'e knew. 'E gave me extra rum.
HARGREAVES   Did you say anything to him?
HAMP   No, sir. Weren't nothing I could expect the like of him to do. Only what he did—giving me extra rum. But he could tell.
HARGREAVES   You were in this state of mind for ten days after the attack, but you stayed put.
HAMP   I knew all the time I were going to do what I did.
HARGREAVES   You what?
HAMP   That were another thing weren't same as any other time afore. I knew sure as death I were goin' to make tracks.
HARGREAVES   You mean you planned it? You made a plan to desert and waited till the opportunity presented itself?
HAMP   No, sir.
HARGREAVES   But what else can I think after what you've said? Remember, I want the truth. Between you and me, the truth—plain, clean, whole truth. Please.
HAMP   It weren't a plan, sir.
HARGREAVES   Why did you wait for ten days?
HAMP   I don't know, sir.
HARGREAVES   Well, let me ask you. Let me put it this way. Surely it was because you were trying to find your courage again. You felt that you couldn't stand any more war. After all, you'd been through as much as any British soldier in France, and what you were feeling was quite natural and understandable, but you were trying, during those ten days, to regain strength to carry on.
HAMP   Maybe that were right, sir. I expect it were.
HARGREAVES   I want you to think about it—get it clearly into your mind. Everyone of us goes through bad times, but you didn't want to be a coward, any more than any of your comrades.
HAMP   Reckon I always were, a bit, sir.
HARGREAVES   So is everybody else.
HAMP   But this were different.

HARGREAVES   You were trying to fight off the panic that overcame you in that shell-hole.

HAMP   If you speak for me, sir, you'll know better nor me what to say.

HARGREAVES   But is that not the truth, or near it?

HAMP   It weren't a plan, sir.

HARGREAVES   Remember that—keep that clear in your mind.

HAMP   I went to the M.O. that time, sir.

HARGREAVES   During those ten days?

HAMP   Yes, sir.

HARGREAVES   Right! Now, this is important. Did you say anything to him then about your state of mind—I mean, the state of your nerves? Was that why you went to him? Who saw you, by the way?

HAMP   It were Captain O'Sullivan himself, sir.

HARGREAVES   And was that why you went? Did you make it clear to him?

HAMP   I told him I couldn't sleep. Neither I could, sir, more'n ten minutes at once. Never like that afore. I told him.

HARGREAVES   Yes? What else?

HAMP   Couldn't eat much neither, sir. I told him that as well.

HARGREAVES   Yes?

HAMP   And I told 'im I couldn't stop shaking.

HARGREAVES   That was true?

HAMP   I wouldn't have said it, sir. I weren't trying anything on, sir, honest.

HARGREAVES   No.

HAMP   Even if I'd have thought of trying it on I wouldn't have said it to *him*, sir, if you understand me. Not Captain O'Sullivan.

HARGREAVES   (*with a half-smile*) Yes, all right. It's just that these details are vitally important. What did Captain O'Sullivan say to you?

HAMP   He give me a number nine, sir. Pills, sir. For me bowels.

HARGREAVES   This was after you'd explained all these symptoms?

HAMP   Yes, sir. I——

HARGREAVES   Yes?

HAMP   I never took it, sir.

HARGREAVES   What?

HAMP   The number nine. I were lucky. He weren't lookin'. I
         spit the pills out when he weren't lookin'. Maybe there
         were *some* kind o' medicine as would've helped me, sir,
         but, one thing I didn't have no call for was a number
         nine. (*This with a half-embarrassed smile.*)
HARGREAVES Did he say anything to you—give you any advice or
         medical instructions?
HAMP   He said I'd cold feet, sir.
HARGREAVES What else?
HAMP   He said a number nine 'ud cure them.
HARGREAVES Anything else?
HAMP   Can't remember no more, sir.
HARGREAVES Now I ask you to think carefully about this next ques-
         tion. Looking back on it, do you not believe that that
         interview with the M.O. must have affected your state
         of mind in an important way? You had gone to him
         for help, as you were quite entitled to do, and if you
         felt you had been badly let down it must have made
         you more confused and desperate than you were before.
         Was that not so?
HAMP   No, sir.
HARGREAVES But surely—surely when all you got out of him was
         some meaningless, stupid cant about—I mean, rightly
         or wrongly, you must have felt badly let down.
HAMP   I didn't expect any different, sir. I didn't expect him to
         say anythin'. Only what he told me.
HARGREAVES Why did you go, then? What did you expect?
HAMP   I were only thinking, like, maybe he would give me
         some kind of medicine as would help me.
HARGREAVES What kind of medicine?
HAMP   Well, I don't know, sir. I thought him bein' the M.O.,
         he would know. I mean, you read about medicine in
         the papers at home.
HARGREAVES You mean some kind of tonic?
HAMP   I forgot the name, sir.
HARGREAVES But that's what was in your mind? A tonic?
HAMP   Aye, sir, that's what they call it. Nerve tonic, like. For
         my nerves. I were hoping he would think on something
         to help my nerves. But he never said.

HARGREAVES However, the point is that you were trying to find something that would bring your morale back.

HAMP Anything that would help me to sleep, sir, and stop me shaking and maybe, like, stop up my diarrhoea.

HARGREAVES Well, yes, all right—that's another way of saying the same thing.

HAMP Course, it wouldn't have made no difference, sir.

HARGREAVES You can't be sure of that, can you?

HAMP No, sir—only——

HARGREAVES Yes?

HAMP I knew all the time I weren't going to go back up the line. I knew I were going to make tracks, like, to get away from it.

HARGREAVES From what exactly?

HAMP Like—the guns, and——

HARGREAVES So you *had* made up your mind to desert?

HAMP No, sir. It's the God's truth I were wanting to stop myself, but it's same as I couldn't help it.

HARGREAVES You knew before you went that the battalion was going to be sent back into the line?

HAMP Yes, sir.

HARGREAVES Was that what finally decided you?

HAMP No, sir.

HARGREAVES Is that true?

HAMP Yes, sir.

HARGREAVES What did decide you, then?

HAMP There weren't nothing special, sir. Only, it were same as this night were the time for it. This night, soon as it got dark, like, I put on a bandolier, took me gas helmet and rifle—let on I had to go on a message—and I just started walking.

HARGREAVES Did you know where you were making for?

HAMP I were walking away from it, sir, that were the most of it.

HARGREAVES Had you any idea in which direction you were going?

HAMP It were the right direction.

HARGREAVES What d'you mean?

HAMP Well, I didn't get stopped. Course, I never got right away from it—not till I got on the train—but the guns were always gettin' further away. It were a daft kind of walkin', because—you'll not believe this, sir, but it's true—after I got a few miles away from the guns I got it into my head I were making for 'ome. Lamton, like. There weren't any sense in it, but it were in my head.

HARGREAVES What happened about the train?

HAMP It were stopped near a level-crossin' when I got there. Middle o' the night by that time. So I jumped on a wagon.

HARGREAVES How did you know the train was going the way you wanted to go?

HAMP I weren't sure. But it were. Coal train. Only stopped once after that. Took me a long way. I slept a while after it got daylight. No sign of guns, an' the sun shining sir. Near Calais, when I wakened up. I never knew at the time, like, but it were near Calais, and the train were slowed down, and the sun still shining. So I jumped off—and that's where they got me, the Redcaps, like, sir.

HARGREAVES What did you tell them, can you remember?

HAMP I said I were goin' on leave.

HARGREAVES Did they believe you?

HAMP No, sir.

HARGREAVES Did you expect them to?

HAMP I thought I would try it. But I didn't have no kit, and then they wanted to see me papers and then they arrested me.

HARGREAVES Did you say anything else to them—any explanation? Did you tell them about your being ill, for instance?

HAMP No, sir.

HARGREAVES Why not?

HAMP I were feeling a lot better by that time.

HARGREAVES What else did they ask you?

HAMP Nothing much.

HARGREAVES Did they say anything to you that you remember?

HAMP Only about me bein' a deserter. And I heard them saying to each other about it being a shooting job.

HARGREAVES Yes?

HAMP They'd never go that length, sir, would they? I mean

shooting like. I don't think there's anybody left in A Company as 'as been out as long as me, sir. They canna shoot me.

HARGREAVES Listen, Hamp, it's my duty to impress the truth on you. You know it but you don't want to believe it. For cowardice in the face of the enemy you *can* be shot.

HAMP I never were a coward before, sir—not any worse nor anybody else. I don't reckon to get off, sir, but——

HARGREAVES You see, I can't dispute the fact that you ran away. You may well be found guilty of desertion—and I'd be failing in my duty if I left any shadow of doubt or vagueness in your mind about what the consequences may be. That's why it's so important that you——

HAMP Same as I were saying, though, sir, I don't reckon to get off, but—I dunna think they'll bother shooting the like o' me.

HARGREAVES I tell you again—military law lays it down quite clearly that— Unless we can convince the Court that you were acting under extraordinary and intolerable strain at the time when you committed this crime you will almost certainly be sentenced to death. Don't you understand that?

HAMP If you tell me, sir. But——

HARGREAVES Yes?

HAMP I mean, this were the first time——

HARGREAVES For the crime of cowardice in battle once is enough. There's another question I have to ask you—I hope you won't mind. It could be quite important. Can you tell me whether there's any history of—nervous illness— mental illness in your family?

HAMP History?

HARGREAVES I mean, any record that you've heard about of——

HAMP You mean, like going off their heads? Daft?

HARGREAVES Well, yes—or——

HAMP No, sir.

HARGREAVES Nothing of that kind at all?

HAMP Not daft, sir, no. Maybe gormless some of them, same as my dad used to say about me, but not daft. I don't think they ever had time, like. Twelve hours a day in t'mills, they wouldn't have time for going off their heads, you might say.

HARGREAVES   Yes, all right. Now, about yourself. Have you—before you joined up—have you had any experience of nervous trouble?

HAMP   No, sir.

HARGREAVES   Extreme anxiety? Depression?

HAMP   Like—getting fed up?

HARGREAVES   Well——

HAMP   I've had that, sir. But nobbut worse nor anybody else that worked along with me. Funny when you think about it now. We never knew when we was well off, like, did we? We never knew what we was in for.

HARGREAVES   We're all in the same boat as far as that's concerned, you know.

HAMP   Yes, sir. That's what I were meaning, sir.

HARGREAVES   Now, before I go, I want to say this to you. You must think very carefully about all the things we've discussed and—even more important—before I see you again try to remember anything else that may have a bearing on your case. I may as well tell you quite frankly we haven't very much to go on so far. So please try to think back before we talk about it again. Try to recall anything in your mind that may have affected your morale. It's very important.

HAMP   Yes, sir. Nothing I can think on right off. I said to you about Willie, sir, didn't I?

HARGREAVES   Willie?

HAMP   Willie Bryson, sir.

HARGREAVES   Oh, yes. About the letter, and——

HAMP   About when he were hit, like, sir. When he were killed.

HARGREAVES   You told me he had been killed.

HAMP   I were along with him at the time.

HARGREAVES   (not too eagerly, having been discouraged so often) Yes?

HAMP   Well, what I mean, sir, you could say that's in my mind —same as you were asking. Like, I don't think as much about it now, but you wouldn't be telling a lie if you said to them it's in my mind.

HARGREAVES   D'you mean this is something that has really worried you—something you don't want to think about but can't keep out of your mind?

HAMP Aye, like that, sir—that's right. Only it's more seeing than thinking.

HARGREAVES Seeing what?

HAMP The way it happened, like.

HARGREAVES This is exactly the kind of thing I mean.

HAMP Well, that's right then, sir.

HARGREAVES (*gently, because he knows it will have to be drawn out*) Listen, I know you don't find it easy to—describe your experiences, but I think you'd better try to tell me more about this.

HAMP I were talking to Willie at the time.

HARGREAVES Yes?

HAMP Course I've seen plenty folk getting killed—same as you have—same as everybody. Hundreds. Thousands. Quick and slow. Weren't the first time neither that I saw somebody getting blown to bits. Bits of nothing, sir—you know what it's like. I've had to wipe and scrape bits off of me afore that an' all—same as everybody else—it weren't the first time. Weren't even same as Willie were anything special to me. Maybe a bit, like, him belonging up our street, but only for that, nothing special. He never had much time for me at home, Willie. I couldn't tell you what kind of—It were quick, of course. Never saw it quicker, never, not for nobody. Couldn't tell you what kind of shell it were. I were nobbut five-six yards away, like, and I were only bleeding—scratches—five-six yards from him—but Willie weren't nowhere—only all over me. Bits. Red and yellow. You know what it's like without me telling you. They had to give me a new uniform. (*Pause.*) Same as I were saying, sir—couldn't tell you what were special about it, but it's the God's truth it's in my mind, like, if that's what you want to know. Not as bad as it was for a while, but——

HARGREAVES Yes. Yes, I understand.

HAMP I'm still seeing it, like, sir, that's what I mean. True, sir.

HARGREAVES Yes. I know. (*Silence as he packs up his notes, etc.*)

Now, listen, there's one more thing I want to ask you—perhaps the most important thing of all. It's about something I'll want to say in court—perhaps ask you there too. Could you be relied on, if the Court were lenient enough to send you to prison, could you be relied upon to do your duty when you came out?

HAMP I would try my best, sir.

HARGREAVES I mean, could you be relied on to go up the line and stay up? I mean exactly that—nothing less. Do you understand me? Do you?

HAMP Yes, sir.

HARGREAVES Well?

HAMP Sir?

HARGREAVES Yes?

HAMP Is there nobbut else for it, sir? Do I have to tell them that?

HARGREAVES Yes. Could you? Could you be relied on?

HAMP I'll say it if you can tell me, sir.

HARGREAVES If I can tell you what?

HAMP If you know any way of being sure, sir.

HARGREAVES Who the hell d'you think I am, man? God Almighty? (*Exit.*)

CURTAIN

ACT II

It is one week later. The scene is the court martial room, which is one of the public rooms of a chateau.
The Court consists of: The President, who is a Brigadier General; a Major, a Captain and two Lieutenants. Also present is CAPTAIN PRESCOTT, *R.F.C., who is the 'Legal Member'.*
The Corporal Guard is in attendance as Court Usher.
HAMP, HARGREAVES *and the Prosecuting Officer,* CAPTAIN MIDGLEY, *are in their appropriate places, and when the curtain rises the* PADRE *is being questioned by* HARGREAVES.

HARGREAVES To sum up, then, Padre—from what you know of the facts of this matter and the character of the prisoner, do you believe that he should be found guilty of desertion?
PADRE No, most certainly not.
HARGREAVES (*sitting down*) Thank you.
PRESIDENT Prosecuting Officer?
MIDGLEY Thank you, sir. (*Then to* PADRE.)
Have you visited the prisoner regularly since his arrest, Padre?
PADRE Yes—as often as I was able to.
MIDGLEY And you've come to know him well?
PADRE I've tried to. And I've tried to help him as much as I could.
MIDGLEY Do you mean in a religious sense?
PADRE Not only in that way, if I understand what you mean. Mainly by encouraging him to talk about his anxieties.
MIDGLEY In particular, perhaps, this charge he was facing?
PADRE Yes, of course.
MIDGLEY Did he talk freely to you about it?
PADRE Yes, he did. But——

MIDGLEY Yes?

PADRE In a sense he doesn't talk freely about anything, least of all I think to—people like you or me.

MIDGLEY You mean he is not very articulate?

PADRE I think it's rather because he is very honest.

MIDGLEY Did you know him well previously—before his arrest?

PADRE Not so well as I do now.

MIDGLEY Did you find him to be a religious man?

PADRE If you're asking whether he had a constant and conscious Christian faith—no, I don't think so.

MIDGLEY And now?

PADRE No.

MIDGLEY I must ask you to answer my next question quite clearly, Padre. Before the time of his arrest, would you say you knew him individually at all?

PADRE I did not intend to imply that I had.

MIDGLEY But surely this must have an important bearing on your answer to Mr. Hargreaves' last question. The case for the prisoner's defence seems to be founded on the assertion that in some way, for some reason not yet made quite clear, he cannot be held fully responsible for the actions which led to his arrest. Surely any opinion about that must depend on a knowledge of the man at that time, and yet you offered a seemingly quite decisive opinion that he is not guilty.

PADRE I don't believe he can be blamed to the extent that the charge states, or to the appalling extent of the penalty it implies.

MIDGLEY I must put it to you, Padre, that the sentence of the court, if he is found guilty, is no concern of yours.

PADRE Can any of us help being concerned?

MIDGLEY Do you feel qualified to give this opinion about his actions at a time when you admit you hardly knew him?

PADRE I know him well enough now to judge what his state of mind must have been.

MIDGLEY Are you sure?

PADRE Yes, quite sure.

C

MIDGLEY   Why, for instance, didn't he come to ask for your help before he went absent? We've been told, as I understand it, that he was in some way mentally disturbed at that time. If he was trying to overcome his attack of 'nerves' weren't you the likeliest person to help him? Isn't that an important part of your job?

PADRE   To patch up cases of damaged nerves and send them back into battle—I suppose that *is* the usual idea of why we're here.

MIDGLEY   Do you not believe it's important? Haven't you done it for other men?

PADRE   Yes, I have. But if I had no better than that to do I would not be here.

MIDGLEY   There is one question I must ask you, Padre. You may feel that it's of rather a private nature, but I consider it fair to ask you. Do you believe it is right that a soldier found guilty of desertion and cowardice in the face of the enemy should be sentenced to death?

PADRE   What if he's driven to an extremity of mental suffering?

MIDGLEY   Do you believe that there are *any* circumstances when it is right?

PADRE   (*compelled to admit*) No—I do not.

MIDGLEY   Can you claim then to offer a fair opinion on this case, within the terms of military law? If you question the assumptions of the law which governs this court, how can you possibly claim to be without prejudice?

PADRE   (*quietly*) This man is not guilty of any crime which justifies your demand for his death.

MIDGLEY   (*interrupting, quietly, knowing he has won, but not gloatingly*) Padre—with respect—I am demanding nothing, except the discovery of the truth and the administering of justice within our law. I'm trying to do my duty.

PADRE   I'm sorry. (*Then accusingly.*) I'm sorry if a Christian faith is a prejudice. In this place at this time perhaps you would wish me to be free of it.

MIDGLEY   Thank you, Padre. There are no more questions from me.

PRESIDENT   Thank you, Padre. If you have no more to say——

(PADRE *steps down.* CORPORAL *opens door for him as he goes out.*)

HARGREAVES   May I have your permission, sir, to make a brief statement, which I hope may save the Court's time?

PRESIDENT   Yes, of course, Mr. Hargreaves.

HARGREAVES   As Defending Officer, sir, I do not intend to dispute the account of Private Hamp's absence from duty which has been presented by the Prosecution. The Prosecuting Officer, if I may presume to anticipate what he will say to you, regards these admitted facts as sufficient in themselves to convict the prisoner of the crime of desertion. My submission, however, is that the act of absenting himself was committed at a time when, because of his state of health—the state, if I may put it in such a way, of his *mental* health—he could not in justice be held responsible for his actions.

PRESIDENT   Mental health, Mr. Hargreaves. It might help us if you could explain more exactly what you mean. Do you mean that the prisoner was or is lunatic?

HARGREAVES   No, sir.

PRESIDENT   Or mentally deficient?

HARGREAVES   No, sir. It is a more difficult question than that. But I hope that the remaining evidence for the defence will make it clear to you what I do mean.

PRESIDENT   Very well. Are you ready for the next witness?

HARGREAVES   Yes, sir.

PRESIDENT   (*consulting list*) Corporal, call Lieutenant Webb.

(CORPORAL *goes to the door and does so. Enter* WEBB. WEBB *is sworn in by* CAPTAIN.)

HARGREAVES   Would you agree, Lieutenant Webb, that conditions in front of St. Julien about the time when this happened were very bad?

WEBB   Yes, pretty bad.

HARGREAVES   A very severe test for even the best of men?

WEBB   Yes.

HARGREAVES   Do you know of anything unusual that happened to the prisoner there?

WEBB   (*hesitates*) D'you mean the shell-hole business?

HARGREAVES   Anything you remember.

WEBB   Well, I've seen it happen before—but it seemed to affect
         him more than—(*Then, to court.*) He got blown into a
         shell-hole, sir—nearly drowned in mud.
PRESIDENT Did you see this happen?
WEBB   Well, just after, sir—after he was pulled out. He was
         pretty nearly done for.
HARGREAVES And is it your opinion that this experience affected him
         very drastically?
WEBB   Yes.
HARGREAVES That after it—as we say—his nerve had gone?
WEBB   Well, yes.
PRESIDENT Did he say anything of the kind to you, Lieutenant
         Webb?
WEBB   No, sir. But——
PRESIDENT I imagine that there would be others of your men in
         much the same condition at that time, were there
         not?
WEBB   Well, none of us were too good, sir, but he must have
         been in a worse way than the rest.
PRESIDENT Why do you say that? Is it because you now know
         what he did?
WEBB   Well, he must have been in a worse way than I could
         see.
PRESIDENT That doesn't necessarily follow. We know what he
         decided to do about it—but we don't know that he was
         in any worse condition than his comrades.
HARGREAVES With respect, sir, I believe I can prove that he was and
         that it's wrong to suppose he 'decided' to do it. If you
         will——
PRESIDENT Nevertheless, Mr. Hargreaves, this distinction must be
         clearly kept in mind. Please continue.
HARGREAVES Was Private Hamp well liked in the platoon?
WEBB   Yes. Always whacked out anything he had. And of
         course he's the nearest we've got now to a founder
         member. He had a name for brewing a good cup of tea
         too.
HARGREAVES What sort of soldier would you say he was before this
         happened?
WEBB   About average, near enough. Nothing special one way

              or the other. Not particularly bright. But one thing about him—he was never a grouser.

HARGREAVES From all your experience of him you regarded him as a reasonable average?

WEBB Yes. He's not a born soldier, but not many of us are.

HARGREAVES Were you surprised when you heard he'd gone absent?

WEBB Yes, I was.

HARGREAVES Can you tell us why?

WEBB It just wasn't like him. He——

HARGREAVES Yes?

WEBB (looking at HAMP) Well, to tell you the truth, I wouldn't have said he had enough gumption to do anything of the kind.

PRESIDENT (sharply) What d'you mean by that, Lieutenant Webb?

WEBB Matter of initiative, sir. He was never known for being very bright in that way. I don't mean any disrespect to him. I've told him the same thing often enough before. (Looking again at HAMP.)

HARGREAVES So you would say that this surprised everybody who knew him?

WEBB Yes. No question about that.

HARGREAVES Because, as you said, it wasn't 'like him'?

WEBB Yes.

HARGREAVES Can you try to explain in more detail?

WEBB Don't know if I can say it any other way.

HARGREAVES Do you mean that it seemed a completely abnormal action on his part?

WEBB Yes, that's right.

HARGREAVES A sign that his mental condition at the time was obviously overwrought—seriously out of balance?

WEBB Yes, it must have been.

HARGREAVES In other words, you believe, from what you knew of him before this happened—and that was how long?

WEBB Couple of years near enough.

HARGREAVES From your knowledge of him over two years, then, you believe that before he would do such a thing he would have to be mentally ill—to some extent out of his mind?

WEBB Yes, I do.

HARGREAVES Thank you. (*To* PRESIDENT.) No more questions, sir.

PRESIDENT Mr. Midgley?

MIDGLEY Thank you, sir. Mr. Webb, about this 'mental illness'—did you see any actual sign of it yourself?

WEBB Well, it depends what you mean.

MIDGLEY Surely if you had it would have been your duty to make sure something was done about it. Did the idea ever occur to you at all before he went absent?

WEBB Well, we didn't have much time for——

MIDGLEY Had the idea occurred to you?

WEBB No, I don't think so, but——

MIDGLEY Is it not, as the President suggested, a matter of trying now to find an excuse for his going absent? Quite natural, of course, to do so, but unless you have evidence of it, it's no business of this court to——

WEBB He could have been—ill—in his mind even if I didn't see it.

MIDGLEY Can you offer any evidence that he was?

WEBB He must have been. He'd had a bad time.

MIDGLEY Had his battle experience not been much the same as the other men in your platoon?

WEBB He's been in it longer than——

MIDGLEY Perhaps longer than the others in your platoon, yes, but surely there are plenty of men in the Company whose service is as long as his and longer?

WEBB I don't know about plenty, but there are some. Anyhow, length of service isn't the only thing that counts. We're not all built the same way. As they say, every man has his own war.

MIDGLEY Yes, I've heard the phrase too, but——

WEBB You know very well it's only one soldier in a thousand who never gets windy.

MIDGLEY Yes, that's exactly what I'm suggesting. Every man, as you say, has his own war, against his own fear. Wouldn't you agree that's what the phrase means?

WEBB That's not what I was getting at.

MIDGLEY Nevertheless, isn't it true? And isn't it true that, however much we may regret it, and however much we may sympathise, isn't it true that this man simply allowed his own fear to become his master, instead of mastering it as his duty required him to do?

WEBB There's a lot more in it than that.

MIDGLEY But—I ask you again—can you recall any evidence to support what you say?

WEBB I've said what I believe.

MIDGLEY Thank you, Lieutenant Webb. (*To* PRESIDENT.) That's all, sir.

(PRESIDENT *nods to* WEBB, *who steps down and goes out. Meanwhile* HAMP *stands up unexpectedly.*)

HAMP Beg pardon, sir.

PRESIDENT Yes?

HAMP Can I speak to the Corporal, sir?

PRESIDENT Yes. All right. Speak up.

HAMP Private, like, sir.

(PRESIDENT, *for the first time uncertain, nods to* COR-PORAL, *who goes over, listens to* HAMP's *whispered request, then goes over to* PRESIDENT *and puts it, still inaudibly, to him.*)

PRESIDENT Why wasn't he taken before?

CORPORAL He was, sir.

HAMP I've got a bit of trouble, sir—last two days.

PRESIDENT Yes. All right. Quick as you can, please.

(CORPORAL *escorts* HAMP *out. Awkward pause.*)

I understand, Mr. Hargreaves, you wish to call only one other witness besides the prisoner himself.

HARGREAVES Yes, sir. Captain O'Sullivan.

PRESIDENT Who is the Company Medical Officer?

HARGREAVES Yes, sir.

PRESIDENT How long do you expect his evidence to take?

HARGREAVES Difficult to say, sir.

PRESIDENT About when do you expect to have your case completed?

HARGREAVES I can't really be sure, sir. It depends on——

PRESIDENT By lunch-time, d'you think?

HARGREAVES By when, sir?

PRESIDENT Lunch-time.

HARGREAVES I may have, but I don't know. (*Then sharply, slightly losing control.*) A man's life is at stake, sir.

PRESIDENT (*after a pause*) I don't think any of us is unaware of that, Mr. Hargreaves. (*Then, after an accusing silence from* HARGREAVES, *he is forced to go on.*) I think perhaps we might have another window open. Getting a bit stuffy.
(LIEUTENANT *moves to open window.*)

HARGREAVES I'm sorry, sir, if I——

PRESIDENT (*to* LIEUTENANT *as he comes back*) Thank you. You will of course be given all the time you require, Mr. Hargreaves.
(HARGREAVES *acknowledges with slight bow of head.*)
We shouldn't complain about the heat, I suppose. Should be thankful to see the sun.

MIDGLEY Yes, I thought that rain would never stop.

PRESIDENT Don't expect it'll be long before we see some more. (*Awkward pause.*) I hope nobody minds?
(*All acknowledge they don't mind the window being open. Pause.* PRESIDENT *looks around.*)
Must have been a fine place in its day.
(*All signify agreement, then conversation dries tensely until footsteps of* HAMP *and* CORPORAL *are heard returning. They come in and return to former positions.*)
Call Captain O'Sullivan, Corporal.

CORPORAL Sir.

PRESIDENT Yes?

CORPORAL I'm not sure if he's come back, sir.

PRESIDENT I thought all the witnesses were reported present before we started.

CORPORAL He was here, sir, but he got called away. They had some more wounded sent down from the line, sir, so I heard.

PRESIDENT Find out whether he has come back, will you?
(CORPORAL *moves to do so, looks, then returns.*)

CORPORAL He's just coming in now, sir.

PRESIDENT Call him, will you?

CORPORAL Captain O'Sullivan.
(*Enter* O'SULLIVAN, *tired-looking, and capless.*)

O'SULLIVAN My apologies, sir. Some very urgent cases.

PRESIDENT Yes, of course.

O'SULLIVAN I've mislaid my cap.

PRESIDENT It doesn't matter. Are you free to give evidence now, d'you think?

O'SULLIVAN Might as well be now, sir.

(PRESIDENT *nods to* CAPTAIN *to administer oath. He does so and* O'SULLIVAN *repeats.* O'SULLIVAN *goes to witness position.*)

HARGREAVES Captain O'Sullivan—as Medical Officer of the prisoner's battalion, do you recall the circumstances of his reporting sick on or about July 18th of this year?

O'SULLIVAN On the 17th. Yes. I looked it up. It's in the book.

HARGREAVES From your records and your own recollection, can you describe what happened?

O'SULLIVAN Very little. Nothing out of the ordinary. The book says M. and D.—Medicine and Duty.

HARGREAVES As clearly as you can remember, what did he complain of?

O'SULLIVAN I remember quite clearly. He complained of nerves.

HARGREAVES Is that how he put it?

O'SULLIVAN More or less.

HARGREAVES May I suggest to you that rather than making a vague general complaint about 'nerves' such as you mention he described certain definite and distressing physical symptoms and asked for your help in relieving them. Did he not tell you, for instance, that he was finding it almost impossible to sleep?

O'SULLIVAN There's nothing in the book about that.

HARGREAVES Is there no recollection of it in your mind?

O'SULLIVAN He may have said something of the kind. I believe he did, now you mention it.

HARGREAVES Did you regard this, in itself or in association with other symptoms, as being in any way serious?

O'SULLIVAN No. If I had I would obviously have made a note of it in the record. It's not uncommon. It's certainly not uncommon for me to be told such things.

HARGREAVES Are you implying that you did not believe what he said?

O'SULLIVAN I'm not implying anything. I'm saying that, like any other Medical Officer, I'm accustomed to hearing complaints of this kind.

HARGREAVES *Did* you believe him?

O'SULLIVAN (*after noticeable pause*) No.

HARGREAVES May I ask why not? For example, can you tell us why you did not believe the prisoner when he said to you that he was suffering from extreme and persistent insomnia?

O'SULLIVAN I don't say I didn't believe that.

HARGREAVES What other symptoms—can you now recall them to mind—did he complain of at the same time?

O'SULLIVAN I think he said he was off his food. And he said he was a bit shaky.

HARGREAVES You mean physically shaky, subject to bouts of uncontrollable trembling?

O'SULLIVAN I don't know about 'uncontrollable'. That's the whole point——

HARGREAVES All right. I don't imagine he would use such a word in any case—but subject to severe bouts of physical trembling. Is that a fair description of what he complained of?

O'SULLIVAN Yes, I suppose so, but——

HARGREAVES Did you believe him in this respect?

O'SULLIVAN It was possible that he had been feeling jumpy—shaky —in that way, but——

HARGREAVES And that he had also been suffering, as he told you, from an inability to eat and sleep normally?

O'SULLIVAN Yes, but——

HARGREAVES Can you tell us, then—you said a moment ago, deliberately and emphatically, that you didn't believe him. Can you tell us now what it was that you did not believe?

O'SULLIVAN I knew what he was after, and——

HARGREAVES With respect, Captain O'Sullivan, that is not an answer to the question. If you didn't believe this man, you must have decided that he was lying.

O'SULLIVAN I didn't believe he had any right to expect from me— what he obviously did expect.

HARGREAVES I must again repeat the question. Did this man tell you any lies, and if so, what were they?

O'SULLIVAN He obviously expected me to relieve him from front-line duty—send him down the line.

HARGREAVES Captain O'Sullivan, did he say so?

O'SULLIVAN Did he what?

HARGREAVES Did he ask you to relieve him from battle-duty?

O'SULLIVAN I didn't need him to tell me what he was after. He wasn't the first one.

HARGREAVES Would it be fair to say that you may now have reconsidered your statement that he lied to you?

O'SULLIVAN I didn't say he lied.

HARGREAVES I put it to you, again, that you said a moment ago you didn't believe this man's story, and you quite clearly conveyed the impression that he lied to you. Will you now either withdraw that allegation or tell us specifically what the lie or lies consisted of?

O'SULLIVAN I think he exaggerated his symptoms.

HARGREAVES (after a pause) How long did your interview with him last?

O'SULLIVAN Five minutes—ten minutes—I couldn't tell you exactly.

HARGREAVES And did you, after the interview, take any steps to investigate this story which you assumed to be an exaggeration of the facts?

O'SULLIVAN No. I couldn't see any need whatever to do anything of the kind. I was quite certain I was right.

HARGREAVES What was the basis of this certainty?

O'SULLIVAN I used my own judgment and experience. Experience of many similar cases.

HARGREAVES In your experience of what you call similar cases, have you ever come to a conclusion different from the one you came to here?

O'SULLIVAN I told you the cases were similar—therefore my judgment of them didn't vary very much.

HARGREAVES And have you prescribed the same treatment in each case?

O'SULLIVAN More or less, yes.

HARGREAVES Laxative pills?

O'SULLIVAN Are you teaching me my job?

HARGREAVES Was the administration of laxative pills in the slightest degree relevant to what was wrong with this man?

O'SULLIVAN I've already told you. I didn't see much wrong with him. He only needed a bit of pulling together.

HARGREAVES Did you suggest or prescribe anything to help him do that?

O'SULLIVAN I talked to him.

HARGREAVES What did you say?

O'SULLIVAN (*sincerely*) Well, I told him he wasn't the first. You may have got the impression I was hard with him, but I wasn't. I didn't shout at him. I listened to what he told me, and even if I had my own reservations about it, I didn't question him. There's no point in going into these things too deeply—it's bad for morale, dangerous. I always try to talk quietly if I can, although it's true with some of them a good dressing-down's more effective, but I decided not with him. Perhaps I was wrong. I don't know, but I decided to talk to him—as far as possible—(*Looking at* HAMP.) man-to-man. Told him he wasn't the first soldier to feel a bit jumpy after a bad time in the line. Told him he'd probably be all right before long—back to normal. Told him to try to get back to normal with his food, try to get some sleep. What else could I say?

HARGREAVES In other words, you gave him a laxative, talked to him for a few minutes, then told him to go away and pull himself together?

O'SULLIVAN I did my job.

HARGREAVES Did it not occur to you—or does it not occur to you now—that his need was for some help and guidance in how to pull himself together?

O'SULLIVAN It's not my job to supply a man with guts if he hasn't got enough of his own.

HARGREAVES Did you consider the possibility that his nervous and mental stability might be seriously disturbed, and that he should be sent down the line for diagnosis by a specialist in that kind of illness?

O'SULLIVAN I did not. Suppose I did think of such a thing, every time a man comes complaining of 'nerves', suppose I did think of sending him down the line for psychological treatment, what d'you think the state and strength of this battalion would be? You can ask me clever questions till you're blue in the face, but I know that illness and lack of guts are two different things. I'm here to fight illness—they have to fight the other thing for themselves. We all have.

HARGREAVES Would you agree that the condition known as shell-shock is an illness?

O'SULLIVAN This was not a shell-shock case.

HARGREAVES It is true, is it not, that shell-shock is recognised by the Army as an illness?

O'SULLIVAN Yes.

HARGREAVES And that one of the symptoms of shell-shock is a state of extreme fear in the presence of gunfire, shell-bursts, and other conditions of battle?

O'SULLIVAN Shell-shock is a different matter altogether.

HARGREAVES Nevertheless, it seems to provide an example of a clear connection between illness and fear, does it not?

O'SULLIVAN I repeat—this was not a case of shell-shock.

HARGREAVES Would you hold a man suffering from shell-shock fully responsible for his actions? Would you, for instance, hold him guilty of cowardice if he showed signs of fear in the course of battle?

O'SULLIVAN Obviously not. But in any case he wouldn't be in battle if he'd been diagnosed as——

HARGREAVES Would you hold him guilty of cowardice or desertion if he turned his back on the battle and ran away in panic?

O'SULLIVAN I tell you he wouldn't be in battle.

HARGREAVES Is there an exact moment in the life of such a man before which he is not suffering from shell-shock and after which he is?

O'SULLIVAN It's quite clear where all this is supposed to be leading, but——

HARGREAVES If a man suffering from shell-shock deserts his duty before his illness is recognised, should he be held guilty of cowardice?

O'SULLIVAN This has nothing whatever to do with what we're supposed to be here for.

HARGREAVES (*to* PRESIDENT) With respect, sir, I suggest that if Captain O'Sullivan answered my questions instead of commenting on them it would save time for all of us, and make it easier for me to show that the questions are relevant. (*Then he loses control for a moment.*) Or perhaps it's precisely because he knows how relevant they are that he's trying to evade them.

PRESIDENT That remark is entirely improper, Mr. Hargreaves.

HARGREAVES (*after a pause to calm down*) My apologies, sir.

PRESIDENT Please proceed. But please take careful note of what I have said.

HARGREAVES (*to* O'SULLIVAN) Does the term 'shell-shock' have a precise medical meaning?

O'SULLIVAN Yes. Of course it has.

HARGREAVES Does it have a unanimously agreed meaning so precise that if, say, you as a doctor were able to maintain constant observation on a man liable to this—illness, you would be able to define the exact moment of time when he began to suffer from it? Is there, in other words, an exact and unanimously agreed boundary line between 'nerves', nervousness, extreme nervousness on the one side, and shell-shock on the other?

O'SULLIVAN My God, man, where the hell d'you think discipline would go if——

HARGREAVES Is there an exact boundary on the one side of which a man is required by Army law to 'pull himself together,' liable to be shot as a criminal if he cannot, and on the other side is given the right to be recognised as suffering from illness? Are you so sure?

O'SULLIVAN (*quietly as always except in one passage mentioned below*) I told you I was quite sure about this case.

HARGREAVES An examination of the kind you have described then, lasting five or ten minutes, is sufficient to leave absolutely no doubt in your mind?

O'SULLIVAN I've told you already it's not my job to maintain a psychological clinic. For one thing, I haven't time for it. God knows you of all people should realise I've more urgent calls on my time. D'you expect me to ask wounded men to wait or let them die while I attend to psychological casualties? In any case, if you'll leave off all this subtle argument just for a minute and think straight about it—suppose I did admit this sort of thing as a proper reason for a man going sick, what d'you think it would do to the morale of the Company? (*Then he loses his temper suddenly.*) I'll tell you this. I not only disagree in my own mind with the line you're taking—I consider I have a duty to resist it! I believe this whole rigmarole of yours here is a ridiculous waste of time—all this damned debating over one miserable —little—when thousands of men are being——

PRESIDENT   Your point of view is understandable, Captain O'Sullivan, but you must realise it is not for you to question the procedure of the court.

O'SULLIVAN   I'm sorry, sir.

HARGREAVES   (*quietly*) I ask you most earnestly, have you not wondered how any man truly in possession of himself, any man who can fairly be held responsible for his actions, could do such desperate, hopeless, stupid things as this man did? I repeat, is it not obvious to you, in all honesty, that these things were done only because he had lost possession of himself?

CAPTAIN   Are you suggesting, Mr. Hargreaves, that desertion—or absence from duty—are you suggesting that we should regard such an action merely as a symptom of illness?

HARGREAVES   No, sir. But——

PRESIDENT   You seem to have come very near to it, I must say.

HARGREAVES   I'm trying, sir, to—because it's my duty here, I'm trying to bring all of us as near as we can get to the truth.

PRESIDENT   We must none of us forget why we are here, Mr. Hargreaves. We are not here primarily to examine the individual character of this man, or even to consider the predicament he finds himself in—now or in the past —however much sympathy we may feel for him. I can understand your obvious concern for the individual man in this soldier's uniform—and remember our law is so concerned for him too—that's why we're here, spared by the Army from its war up there. But the law must also be concerned with him as a soldier—*and* concerned for his comrades. I can understand why you have appealed to our sympathy for the man who is here within our sight, but it is our duty to resist your appeal and reach a just verdict not only about this man, but about this soldier and about what this soldier has done. Have you any more questions for Captain O'Sullivan?

HARGREAVES No, sir.

PRESIDENT Mr. Midgley?

MIDGLEY Yes, sir, if you please. (*To* O'SULLIVAN.) Have any of the Defending Officer's questions altered the conclusion you reached about the prisoner when he reported to you on July 17th?

O'SULLIVAN No.

MIDGLEY In view of all the psychological speculation we have heard, and which may have tended to obscure our recollection of it, will you recall in your own words what that conclusion was?

O'SULLIVAN I found the prisoner fit for duty provided he was kept under discipline and discouraged from malingering.

MIDGLEY Did you form the opinion that he was inclined to, as we say, cold feet?

O'SULLIVAN Yes. ,

MIDGLEY And you consider it an important part of your duty to discourage this kind of thing firmly?

O'SULLIVAN Yes.

MIDGLEY And there is nothing you would wish to add to your judgment now by way of qualification?

O'SULLIVAN Nothing whatever.

MIDGLEY Thank you, Captain O'Sullivan.
(*Exit* O'SULLIVAN.)

HARGREAVES (*to* PRESIDENT) May I take evidence now from the prisoner, sir?

PRESIDENT Yes. (HAMP *takes the oath.*)

HARGREAVES Private Hamp, will you simply tell us in your own words what you wish the court to know?

HAMP About the shell-hole, sir?

HARGREAVES Yes, begin there if you like.

HAMP (*who has obviously, although not too obviously, memorised this, and starts off quite well*) Well, I were all right before that, sir, but when I got knocked in there after the whizzbang came over I—I went in deep. It were same as I couldn't find no bottom to it.

HARGREAVES Yes?

HAMP Well, it came over me I weren't going to get out of it. It were same as some boggarts'd got hold of my legs, pullin' me down, like. And me not even wounded, but that were the worst bit of it—not even wounded, but I were goin' to get choked to death. Same as something were after me, special like, sir.

HARGREAVES What did you do?

HAMP I couldn't do nothing, sir. Tried to shout and scream but I couldn't get it out. Same as I were up against something I couldn't fight.

PRESIDENT But surely you'd been in considerable danger before. You'd probably even been caught in shell-hole mud before, hadn't you?

HAMP Yes, sir.

PRESIDENT I don't quite follow why this was so different.
(HAMP *is of course very much less fluent in dealing with anyone other than* HARGREAVES.)

HAMP It were, sir. It were something special, same as I said.

PRESIDENT But why?

HAMP Same as there were boggarts in there, sir.

HARGREAVES (*to* PRESIDENT) Devils, sir. North-country word.

PRESIDENT But surely the fact that you were pulled out safely must have rid your mind of any such nonsense?

HAMP Yes, sir.

PRESIDENT Well? Didn't it?

HAMP I were only saying what I had in my head at the time, sir—same as Mr. Hargreaves told me——

PRESIDENT Is this what made you go absent?

HAMP It were same as that started it, sir, I think. But——

PRESIDENT *Did* this idea, that—devils were after you—did it stay in your mind after you were rescued from the mud?

HAMP Not the same, sir. Not much.

PRESIDENT Well, then. What do you think did make you run away?

HAMP I don't know, sir, not rightly. I couldn't stand it no more, I can't rightly say it. Mr. Hargreaves can tell you better.

PRESIDENT Mr. Hargreaves has asked you to tell us, in your own way.

D

HAMP   If you let him ask me, sir, I——

PRESIDENT It's my duty to ask you too, if I think your answers are not sufficiently clear.

HAMP   Yes, sir. Only I'm not very good at it.

PRESIDENT No. Carry on then, Mr. Hargreaves, please.

HARGREAVES Did you realise what you were doing when you left the battalion that night?

HAMP   (*unconvincing, because he doesn't really understand*) No, sir. I don't think so, sir. I——

HARGREAVES D'you mean that you weren't fully in your right mind?

HAMP   (*loyally*) That's what it was, sir.

HARGREAVES (*desperately*) Were you worried about your wife?

HAMP   Yes, sir.

HARGREAVES Will you tell the Court why?

HAMP   Well, I—I got a letter.

PRESIDENT Yes?

HAMP   Well, it were to tell me she's been carrying on a bit— with some other chap, like.

HARGREAVES (*after waiting*) And this was preying on your mind?

HAMP   Well, it were a bit, like, sir.

HARGREAVES When you went absent, were you really conscious of what you were doing? Or was it as if you were being compelled to do it?

HAMP   Yes, sir. I think it were—same as you said.

HARGREAVES I mean, it's not true, is it, to say that you *decided* to desert, deliberately decided—prepared to risk the consequences, but hoping to get away with it?

HAMP   I weren't thinking much at the time, sir.

HARGREAVES No, exactly. And——

HAMP   (*remembering the phrase*) Didn't have no plan in my mind.

HARGREAVES (*more hopefully*) Had you any idea where you were going?

HAMP   I were only wantin' to get left alone for a bit, sir, that's all.

HARGREAVES Did you——?

PRESIDENT You say you wanted to be left alone 'for a bit'. Does that mean you intended to go back to the battalion?

HAMP   *(after looking helplessly at* HARGREAVES) I don't know, sir.

PRESIDENT   This is a very important question, Private Hamp. I can't emphasise too much how important it is. Did you intend to return to the battalion?

HAMP   *(in great difficulty)* Honest to God, sir, I—I can't say.

HARGREAVES   *(sudden outburst)* My God, can't you see it's because he didn't know what he was doing. He doesn't know how to lie to you. *(Then he turns to* HAMP, *and asks very gently.)* Wasn't it simply because you can't clearly remember?

HAMP   That's right, sir.

HARGREAVES   And likewise you can't clearly remember why you went absent—because, as you say, there wasn't any clear reason or plan in your mind at all, was there?

HAMP   That's right, sir. Didn't have no plan. It were same as I just started goin', sir, makin' tracks, because I couldn't stop myself.

PRESIDENT   Did you try to stop yourself?

HAMP   I couldn't sir, that's all. *(To* HARGREAVES.) Same as you told me to say, sir, I couldn't help it. It were same as some way—I were made to—*(Then, after struggling.)* That's all I can say, sir. I can't think of no more. Only——

HARGREAVES   Yes?

HAMP   Well, can I ask you something, sir?

HARGREAVES   *(to* PRESIDENT) Sir?

PRESIDENT   Yes, carry on.

HAMP   *(to* HARGREAVES) Well, it were only to ask you, sir—I would sooner if you could tell them. You know more about it than me——

PRESIDENT   Have you any other questions, Mr. Hargreaves?

HARGREAVES   No, thank you, sir.

PRESIDENT   Mr. Midgley?

MIDGLEY   *(to* HAMP) Did you know you were doing wrong when you deserted?

HAMP   I never thought much on it, sir.

MIDGLEY   But you must surely have been aware of it all the time at the back of your mind?

HAMP If anybody'd tried to stop me I'd have stayed, sir.

MIDGLEY But didn't you wait till you'd made sure there was nobody there to stop you?

HAMP I think I were just lucky, sir, getting away, like.

MIDGLEY (*rather sadly*) That's very much a matter of opinion—whether you were lucky or not in being allowed to desert your duty. But what I'm asking is this. You did know, didn't you, that it was your duty to stay with the battalion?

HAMP Yes, sir.

MIDGLEY And you must have been quite aware of that in your mind during all the time when you were absent—from the very first moment when you deserted?

HAMP I don't know, sir. It's a long while ago.

MIDGLEY I'm asking you to remember, and tell the truth about it.

HAMP But I told them already, sir. It were same as I couldn't stay. I can't tell it no different. I can't remember nothing else in my mind, and that's the God's truth, sir.

MIDGLEY But you could walk, and speak, and think, like anybody else. And you managed to get quite a long way away before you were captured.

HAMP Same as I said, though, sir—I were only lucky.

MIDGLEY Let me put it to you quite simply. Did you know what you were doing?

HAMP Yes, sir. But I couldn't help myself.

MIDGLEY And you knew your comrades were staying at their posts, prepared to do their duty while you were deserting them? Didn't you? Didn't you?

HAMP (*after a pause—beaten*) I never did the like of this before, sir, never. This were the very first time.

MIDGLEY (*to* PRESIDENT) That's all, sir.

PRESIDENT Mr. Hargreaves, I take it you wish to address the court now on the prisoner's behalf.

HARGREAVES Yes, sir. Sir, the battle which is going on within our hearing is the same battle of Passchendaele, now prolonged by many months, in which this man was wounded—yes, I say wounded—rendered incapable of carrying on with his duty just as surely as if a bullet or a piece of shrapnel had entered his body. We are concerned here with a question of responsibility. I believe it is something about which we are only now beginning to learn a little wisdom—I mean the extent to which a man may be blamed, or should be punished, for such things as Captain O'Sullivan calls 'lack of guts'. It has been suggested, sir, that it is a dangerous question. Perhaps it is, in this place at this time—but I believe that the example you are now considering is so extreme that there is no question about it. Can any of you say, knowing what you now know of this man, that when he left his place of duty his mind was not maimed by war? Concern for or about the individual man is, as you say, only part of what you must keep in mind, but your judgment today must surely turn on your instinctive feelings about what sort of man this is. Is he crafty? Cunning? A liar? Always ready with a glib answer? God knows, I could have wished many times this morning that he *had* been more ready with his answers—perhaps even a few lies. But this is a man who is incapable of cunning or lying, even to save his own skin. You must surely have seen that today. Therefore when he says quite simply that 'he couldn't stand any more war' in that place at that time it means no more and no less. He could not. Because he had been maimed in battle—maimed by many battles, the question of yes or no, courage or cowardice, had gone beyond his responsibility, and, I believe, beyond our right to make a sacrifice of him. If we do, I believe it will be on our consciences for the rest of our lives.

PRESIDENT (*very formally*) Thank you. Mr. Midgley, do you wish to address the court?

MIDGLEY No, thank you, sir.

PRESIDENT Mr. Prescott, will you as the Representative detailed by the Judge Advocate General's Department advise us on the law as it applies to this case?

PRESCOTT The court will remember that the soldier takes the law of England with him wherever he goes; Hong Kong, Flanders or elsewhere. It is not his task to prove himself innocent but the prosecution's to prove him guilty. If

the members of the court have any reasonable doubt—
although it must not of course be a fanciful doubt—they
must give him the benefit of it. You will remember that
you have had before you the opinion of the battalion
medical officer, which is that at the time the prisoner
left the battalion he was not shell-shocked but only
suffering from what the doctor described as 'cold feet'
and was fit for duty. You must not be unduly swayed by
the eloquence of the Defending Officer, who has quite
properly made out the best case he can. If you doubt
that the prisoner really meant to desert and you believe
he merely went absent without leave and intended to
return after a few days, you will give a verdict accord-
ingly. On the other hand, if you are satisfied he really
deserted, it is your duty to find him guilty. As to the
emphasis which earlier in the trial the Defending Officer
placed on the fact that the prisoner is a volunteer, you
must not be unduly influenced by that. The army is now
composed of regulars, of volunteers, and of conscripts,
and one law applies to them all. It is the court's duty to
administer the law as it stands.

PRESIDENT (*after consultation with colleagues*) Corporal.

CORPORAL Sir.

PRESIDENT Call the Guard. The prisoner is to be kept in their charge
until we recall him.

(CORPORAL *calls* GUARD, *and they go through drill
required for getting* HAMP *out.*)

Gentlemen, for the sake of privacy we propose to use
the smaller room next door for our discussion of the
case. You will, of course, remain within call. (*He rises,
followed by the others.*) Thank you both for your
help.

(*They go out through connecting door behind their
table.* MIDGLEY *goes out through central door, leaving*
HARGREAVES *alone. As he broods over his notes,* WEBB
comes in.)

WEBB Well?

HARGREAVES Hello, Tom.

WEBB How did he behave?

HARGREAVES   That one doesn't behave, Tom. He just goes on being
             what he is. God help him.
      WEBB   He didn't do very well for himself, then?
HARGREAVES   As well as he could, I suppose.
      WEBB   They don't tell us today, do they?
HARGREAVES   No. It goes for confirmation. C.-in-C.
      WEBB   Best thing you can do is forget about it till then.
HARGREAVES   At least—we *shouldn't* know today, but we probably
             will, to tell you the truth.
      WEBB   You mean from the look on their faces? I wouldn't be
             too sure with that lot.
HARGREAVES   No, it's something I've heard about—something to look
             out for. I'm not supposed to know, but I wrote to a chap
             I know in the other company. Remembered he'd done
             a defence not so long ago—same kind of case.
      WEBB   Been a lot of them lately?
HARGREAVES   That's what our President said to me just before this one
             —by way of encouragement I suppose.
      WEBB   What happened with the other one?
HARGREAVES   They won. At least, he got a year in the glasshouse.
             A.W.L.
      WEBB   He's all right.
HARGREAVES   Anyhow, what I found out, on the day of the court,
             after they've decided the verdict, if they don't ask for
             the conduct sheet, your man's all right. If they do, he's
             for it.
      WEBB   Hamp won't know anything about this, though?
HARGREAVES   I'd sooner I didn't either.
      WEBB   I thought we could shelve it for a few days.
HARGREAVES   I haven't told anyone else. Didn't know whether to
             mention it to you or not. Thought I would tell you
             afterwards if it was all right.
      WEBB   And if it wasn't you'd keep it to yourself.
HARGREAVES   I didn't know.
      WEBB   You've been keeping too much of this to yourself. D'you
             know what I'd do? I'd send the poor sod back up the
             line and hope he gets a packet.
HARGREAVES   Hope?
      WEBB   Well, he deserves it, doesn't he?

HARGREAVES If you believe that what the hell's the point of——?

WEBB We haven't very much bloody option, have we? Or there's going to be a hell of a lot more of us trying the same dodge he tried.

HARGREAVES It's not as simple as that. You know it's not.

WEBB It's got to be simple.

HARGREAVES You think O'Sullivan was quite right then?

WEBB Listen, why don't we just admit when there's nobody listening—friend Hamp was no more off his head than you or me? He'll tell you himself—he hasn't the bloody sense to go off his head.

HARGREAVES So he was just a plain coward?

WEBB Christ, I don't know if he has the sense to be that either.

HARGREAVES That's the real trouble, isn't it? You can't call him any names. He's just bloody Hamp. He can't help it. Never pretended to be anything else.

WEBB Well, if you want an argument, the army can't help being the army.

HARGREAVES I suppose there was something he pretended.

WEBB Aye—to be a bloody soldier. So the army's entitled to call him names. If he's a coward they're entitled to call him a coward.

HARGREAVES But you know better.

WEBB I know, same as you—he's gormless—done—useless.

HARGREAVES So the army's entitled to shoot him?

WEBB Yes, because it's infectious.

HARGREAVES D'you think he deserves to be shot?

WEBB Listen, Bill, I don't want an argument. You're getting into this too deep for your own good.

HARGREAVES Do you, though?

WEBB Of course I do. So do you. You'd better. Doing your job to help him, that's one thing, but——

HARGREAVES D'you like him?

WEBB Do I what? What the hell's liking him got to do with it?

HARGREAVES I just wondered.

WEBB He's a bloody nuisance. That's all he is.

HARGREAVES If you were on the court martial would you find him guilty?

WEBB   I expect so.

HARGREAVES   Why did you try to help him as a witness?

WEBB   Because he would be a hell of a lot less of a nuisance to me if he got off. Remember, I've got a selfish interest in this, haven't I? Top of the list for bloody executioner if it's on.

(*Door opens. Enter* CORPORAL OF GUARD.)

CORPORAL   (*to* HARGREAVES) Sir, I don't know if it's allowed, but he says he would like to see you.

HARGREAVES   What do you think, Tom?

WEBB   Can't do any harm, can it?

HARGREAVES   Bring him in, Corporal.

(CORPORAL *goes out.*)

WEBB   Now remember—no bloody sympathy.

(CORPORAL *and* HAMP *enter.*)

HARGREAVES   (*rather severely*) Yes, Hamp?

HAMP   I hope it weren't wrong, sir—me askin' you to speak up for me, like. I couldn't remember all you told me.

HARGREAVES   No—that's all right.

WEBB   Straighten your back, man. You're supposed to be standing to attention.

HAMP   (*doing so*) Sir.

HARGREAVES   Anything else you wanted to say?

HAMP   Well, I were wantin' to thank you, sir—in case I—well, I expect I'll be going to the glasshouse, shan't I? And in case I might not see you again for a while.

HARGREAVES   Of course you'll see me.

WEBB   Don't be a bloody fool, man.

HARGREAVES   We don't know where you're going, if you're going anywhere. I've explained to you several times—we won't know what the court's verdict is, not for three or four days probably.

HAMP   Well, it were just in case, sir. Wouldn't like to miss thankin' you.

HARGREAVES   Yes, all right.

HAMP   You—haven't heard anything, have you, sir?

HARGREAVES   (*ominously*) No—I've told you, man.

HAMP   I were only wondering, sir. But after what you said they couldn't help but——

HARGREAVES Listen, Hamp, if there's nothing more urgent than this you have to say you'd better get back to——

HAMP What I mean though, sir, beggin' your pardon. It were true, that's what I mean—nearly all you said to them. I could never've said it.

HARGREAVES It was my job to say it.

WEBB If you'd remembered your job none of this blasted rigmarole would have been needed—can't you get that into your head, man?

HAMP Yes, sir.

HARGREAVES This isn't a bloody game, you know.

HAMP It's not same as I haven't thought about it, sir. I have— honest. I know the way it could turn out. I'm only hopin'—that's what I mean. And Lieutenant Hargreaves —he made the best of it—I were only wantin' to tell him he's been very good to me. Wouldn't have no chance if it wasn't for him. But I were only tryin' to look on the cheery side—no sense doin' anythin' else.

HARGREAVES All right. And thank you. Now you'd better go back if there's nothing more. We'll see you later.

HAMP Yes, sir. (*Then, as he is about to be taken away.*) In case I forget, sir, Corporal here got a message from them in there.

CORPORAL It's nothing important, sir. I would have told you.

HAMP Well, I were thinking maybe it's—like, quite a good sign —them wanting to see what's been put down about me before. I mean, same as you said to them, there's not been much against me.

HARGREAVES What was the message?

HAMP Well, Corporal says they want to see my conduct sheet, like, sir.

CURTAIN

ACT III

SCENE I

Two weeks later. The barn as in Act One. Night. HAMP *is alone, playing his mouth organ in exactly the same position as when the play opened. After a few moments, during which we hear distant gunfire and sounds of marching infantry, the* CORPORAL OF THE GUARD *comes in. He stops outside the door of the barn and calls inside.*

CORPORAL Arthur.
         (HAMP *doesn't hear.*)
         (*More loudly.*) Arthur!
HAMP Hello? Is it you, Corp?
CORPORAL Aye.
HAMP Coming in?
CORPORAL Aye—in a minute. Just waiting for Charlie.
         (*Looking back.*) We've got——
HAMP Any word of our lads back?
CORPORAL Aye. They're coming in. Your lot's back this last hour.
HAMP How did they go?
CORPORAL Bad enough, so I hear. Just about the usual. Listen, Arthur—Charlie and the lads—they've been saving up some rum, like—and——
HAMP Oh aye?
CORPORAL Got quite a drop of good stuff saved up, and they were thinking—mebbe a bit of a sing-song tonight.
HAMP Aye—that would be fine.
         (*Enter* GUARD.)
GUARD (*quietly*) Corp.
CORPORAL I thought you were bringing it, Charlie. Where's the rest of them?

GUARD No, listen, Corp. Come here.

CORPORAL Hold on a minute, Arthur, will you?

(HAMP *resumes playing.*)

GUARD (*as* CORPORAL *goes over to him*) They've had word through. I thought I'd better let you know, Corp, before——

CORPORAL Who told you?

GUARD Young Danny—says he got it straight from a bloke in the Orderly Office.

CORPORAL Definite?

GUARD Aye, it sounds like it.

CORPORAL When?

GUARD Well, they say it's to be in the morning.

CORPORAL This bloke in the Orderly Office—did he see it?

GUARD Aye—he got a look, so Danny said.

CORPORAL Tomorrow morning?

GUARD Half past six.

CORPORAL Jesus Christ.

GUARD Course, he knows already, doesn't he? I mean, he's waiting for it. He knew it was coming.

CORPORAL He's waitin' for nothing. He's just going on. He didn't believe it—you know that bloody fine—even after they told him. Jesus Christ.

GUARD Who tells him?

CORPORAL I don't know. Some bastard.

GUARD They've got to tell him now, haven't they? I mean they've got to give him time.

HAMP You there, Corp?

CORPORAL Aye, comin', Arthur. (*To* GUARD.) You come in along wi' me, Charlie.

GUARD You're not for telling him, are you?

CORPORAL What the hell d'you think I am?

(*They go into barn.*)

HAMP Was that all you heard, Corp?

CORPORAL What about?

HAMP About the lads. Have you seen any of them?

CORPORAL No.

HAMP Did you hear anything about Mr. Hargreaves?

GUARD Aye—he's back. Webb as well.

HAMP Expect I'll see them. Just wondering if they'll maybe have any word—where I'm gettin' sent to, like.

CORPORAL I was thinking, Arthur—that place we've got, next to the Guard Room—it's warmer than this; Charlie was saying we should bring you there an' we'll all have a drink.

HAMP You'll be in trouble.

CORPORAL Ah, to hell.

HAMP Well, if you're laying it down, like.

CORPORAL Aye, come on.

HAMP If they come with any word—like, Mr. Hargreaves or any of them——

CORPORAL They'll know where to look, Arthur.

HAMP Aye. (*As they go out.*) Only I didn't want to get you into trouble. Will I bring me mouth organ?

CORPORAL Aye. What the hell d'you think we want you for? (HAMP *goes back for it.*)

HAMP What's the rum saved up for, then? Is it somebody's birthday, like?
(*They go out. Pause. Then* HARGREAVES, WEBB *and* PADRE *come in—wordlessly, until they are inside the barn.*)

WEBB (*to* PADRE) Did you see the order?

PADRE Yes. It was really just a repeat of the last message—except of course we can't go any further this time.

HARGREAVES Do they give any reason?

WEBB To hell, Bill, it's all been gone into before.

PADRE (*bitterly*) 'Danger of rot setting in.'

WEBB Of course it's true enough.

PADRE Is it?

WEBB They have to draw the line somewhere. The way they look at it it's a clear case.

HARGREAVES Have you been told officially yet, Tom?

WEBB Yes. I'm on it.

HARGREAVES They don't waste much time once it's final, do they?

WEBB Better that way.

HARGREAVES Do you believe it?

WEBB What?

HARGREAVES That it can possibly happen?

WEBB Look, Bill, I'm not for bloody well talking about it. There's been too much talking already.

HARGREAVES Who tells him?

WEBB The Orderly Officer. It's laid down.

(Bring in sound of distant singing from here on.)

HARGREAVES Can't they let him have his sleep first?

WEBB No—it's got to be done tonight.

HARGREAVES I suppose it's better.

WEBB He still won't believe in it anyway, you wait. God knows he's been told definitely enough already—it was only a question of when, but he still managed to expect it would be all right.

PADRE He must be helped to prepare for it.

WEBB Have you been seeing him?

PADRE Yes, of course.

WEBB Has he got any religion?

PADRE I've been trying to get him into a proper frame of mind, but I haven't been very good at it.

HARGREAVES Nobody has.

PADRE He's not ready yet.

HARGREAVES Will you be staying with him through the night?

PADRE Of course, yes, if he's willing. And I'll thank God for the chance.

WEBB I've been thinking about it too. I've laid on a couple of things that might be very useful—although *(To* PADRE.*)* I don't know how the idea'll strike you.

PADRE What things?

WEBB Rum—and morphia.

PADRE It's not for me to say. I've no more experience of this than you. We're all trying to find our way.

HARGREAVES We'd better get him back here, hadn't we? He'd better be here when they come. *(Going to bell rope.)* Does this thing still work?

WEBB I expect so.

*(*HARGREAVES *pulls bell.)* Stupid bloody noise.

*(*HARGREAVES *again pulls the bell. This time the singing begins to tail off and dies in mid-song.)*

PADRE I spoke to the C.O. about spirits. It's left to his discretion, and he's left it to me. Apparently there's no objection if the prisoner makes himself insensible beforehand.

(*The* CORPORAL *approaches and comes through door.*)

CORPORAL Sir.

HARGREAVES Where is he, Corporal?

CORPORAL We've got him with us, sir. We thought he could do with——

HARGREAVES Yes, all right. You've heard the news, I suppose?

CORPORAL Yes, sir. Not him of course, sir.

HARGREAVES No. He's to be told soon. I'm sorry, but you'd better get him back here now, I think.

CORPORAL Yes, sir. (*Exit.*)

WEBB What else did the C.O. say to you?

PADRE Everything's been arranged to make it as quick as possible. And—about morphia—he's left that to me too. The M.O.'s empowered to do whatever is requested.

WEBB I'd sooner do it myself. I know what to do—used to be in the R.A.M.C. Anyhow, I think I've a right to do it.

PADRE Yes, all right.   ·

HARGREAVES All very efficient. Nothing seems to have been forgotten.

PADRE Only mercy. .

(*Enter* SERGEANT MAJOR *and young* ORDERLY OFFICER.)

ORD. OFF. (*to* HARGREAVES) I understood the prisoner would be here, sir.

HARGREAVES He's been—he's just being brought back.

ORD. OFF. (*showing paper*) I have to read this to him.

HARGREAVES Yes, I know. We'll stay, if you don't mind.

(ORDERLY OFFICER *nods.*)

WEBB Not me. Better go and pick up these supplies. What's the time?

HARGREAVES Just after nine.

WEBB Back in five minutes.

(*He goes out, but as he does so* CORPORAL *and* HAMP *come in.*)

HAMP (*to* HARGREAVES) Is it—word, like, sir?

SERG. MAJOR Prisoner—shun!

ORD. OFF. Private A. Hamp, Number 873426, it is my duty to inform you that the General Officer Commanding in

Chief has decided that the sentence passed on you by a Field General Court Martial to suffer death by being shot for desertion is to be carried out on Thursday, September 16th at 05.30 hours.

HAMP *(after a silence, to* HARGREAVES*)* When's that, sir?

HARGREAVES Tomorrow.

PADRE Tomorrow morning.

HAMP Are they goin' to do it, then?

HARGREAVES It's been ordered. There's nothing else for it.

PADRE There's nothing else now but prepare for it. We can help you to prepare for it.

ORD. OFF. The C.O. says he's to have everything he wants.

PADRE *(to him,* SERGEANT MAJOR *and* CORPORAL*)* Yes. You can leave him with us now.
(All three go out.)

HARGREAVES *(pouring drink from flask to cup)* Here, drink this, lad. Sit down.

PADRE *(putting arm round* HAMP's *shoulder)* First of all you must realise that this is true. You must accept it and try to prepare yourself for it. You can if you're willing. Will you try?
*(*HAMP *is silent, beyond communication.)*
Will you let me try to help you?
(Again silence.)
I think I can if you'll listen and talk with me.
(Again silence.)
Listen. Please try to listen. The mistake we all make is to expect life to be anything but hard and tough, for what we go through here's only the try-out for the next life—God seeing what we're made of, whether we deserve the reward we'll get if we do our best.

HAMP Yes, sir.

PADRE All of us here in this battle—or anywhere, even at home —we know we may have to die any time. You and me and Lieutenant Hargreaves there, we've been close to death a hundred times. So it's no new thing for the likes of us, we know it well. At this very minute, up yonder, men are dying. All through this night and tomorrow there will be—plenty of others to keep you company.

And then lads you know who've gone already. They
know you and you know them; they understand. Best
of all, God understands—and He loves you. And Jesus
who came down to this miserable, tormented world to
save sinners like you and me, Jesus loves you.

HAMP   Yes, sir.

PADRE   So you see there's nothing much to fear, not much more
than you've faced up to many a time before, for we've
all been in places we never expected to come out of
alive, aye, many and many a time. My son, do you
understand what I'm trying to say to you?
(HAMP *still completely silent, but holds out cup to* HAR-
GREAVES *silently asking for more.* HARGREAVES *pours
and hands it back.* PADRE *goes on.*)
Try and look at it this way; there's so much in life none
of us can fathom, only God Himself understands.

HAMP   (*to* HARGREAVES) Sir.

HARGREAVES   Yes?

HAMP   I need to go some place, sir.

HARGREAVES   Yes, of course. All right.
(*He pulls bell-rope. Silence. Enter* CORPORAL.)

CORPORAL   Sir.

HARGREAVES   Latrine, Corporal.

CORPORAL   Yes, sir.
(*Exeunt.*)

PADRE   What can I say to him?

HARGREAVES   (*bitterly*) Well, there's certainly no point in apologising
to him. He believes it now—that's quite an achievement
in itself.
(*Enter* WEBB, *with bag from which during the following
he takes bottles of rum, a mug, and medical syringe.*)

WEBB   How is the poor bastard? Sorry, Padre, but——
(PADRE *shakes his head, indicating that there is no need
to apologise.*)

HARGREAVES   He hasn't told us.

WEBB   Well, I've seen O'Sullivan—got this out of him. (*Showing syringe.*) He didn't like the idea, but he liked it a
lot better than doing it himself. There's enough here and
more to put a man out for twenty-four hours. Saw the

Sergeant Pioneer too, by the way—arranged for rope and a chair to lash him on to. Might as well do that before we take him out. He'll have to be carried out anyhow—and he'll have to be lashed on to something upright for the shooting. At least, that's if—what d'you think, Padre?

PADRE   Yes. I think you're right about the morphia. I shouldn't say it, but I can't see any other way. But will you let me try to give him communion first?

WEBB   That's your department. But I think after that the sooner the better.

PADRE   Yes. There isn't any right way.

WEBB   (*to* HARGREAVES) What the hell are you looking at me like that for?

HARGREAVES   Do you believe it's going to happen? Do you believe you're going to do it?

WEBB   All right, I'll tell you. Once. This is the worst bloody thing ever, but I can't see any difference between doing it and watching it. Maybe better get it to do—make sure nobody else makes a muck of it—I like things practical, all right? There are different ways of trying to help him, you know.

(*The* PADRE *meanwhile has been laying out an altar cloth, and* HARGREAVES *now pours a drink for* WEBB *and tries to hand it to him.*)

No thank you.

(*Enter* HAMP *and* CORPORAL.)

CORPORAL   (*to* HARGREAVES) He's a bit better now, sir.

HAMP   I were a bit ill, sir, but I'm all right.

WEBB   (*has poured rum*) Have some of this, lad.

(HAMP *takes it.*)

HARGREAVES   (*to* HAMP) Are you sure?

HAMP   (*almost with a smile*) Aye, sir. I'm not much used to it, but it's good medicine. I'll be better of it.

WEBB   Drink up.

(HAMP *does. A long pull.*)

HAMP   (*to* HARGREAVES) Did you think you'd got me off, sir?

HARGREAVES   I tried to tell you there wasn't much hope that the verdict would be changed.

HAMP   I were sure you would manage it, sir. I were sweating on it. I don't mind telling you I never thought they would go to the bother of this. (*Another pull.*) I reckon it'll be quick, sir?

HARGREAVES   Yes.

HAMP   D'you reckon it's fair?

HARGREAVES   (*after a silence*) I don't know. It's not for me to say.

HAMP   I could've been still working at home. Same as you said to them—I weren't made to come here.

HARGREAVES   Would you like to write any letters?

HAMP   Me, sir?

HARGREAVES   Would you like me to write them for you?

HAMP   My mother, sir. An' t'wife. Might as well. Will you write after?

(WEBB *refills mug.*)

HARGREAVES   Yes, of course.

HAMP   What'll you tell them, though?

HARGREAVES   I'll say you died like a soldier.

HAMP   It's not true, sir.

HARGREAVES   It could be.

HAMP   I'll try my best. (*Another pull.*) I will.

PADRE   Will you take communion?

HAMP   If you like, sir.

(PADRE *directs* HAMP *to kneel at the table.*)

PADRE   We do not presume to come to this thy Table, O Lord, trusting in our own righteousness, but in thy manifold and great mercies.

Thou art the same Lord, whose property is always to have mercy.

Grant us therefore, gracious Lord, so to eat the flesh of thy dear Son Jesus Christ, and to drink his blood, that our sinful bodies may be made clean by his body, and our souls washed through his most precious blood, and that we may evermore dwell in him.

My son, despise not thou the chastening of the Lord, nor faint when thou art rebuked of him. For whom the Lord loveth he chasteneth, and scourgeth every son whom he receiveth.

Our Lord Jesus Christ, who has left power to His Church

to absolve all sinners who truly repent and believe in
Him, of His great mercy forgives thee thine offences,
and by His authority committed to me, I absolve thee
from all thy sins—in the name of the Father, of the Son,
and of the Holy Ghost.

(HAMP's *head has been gradually falling lower and
lower, and is now resting insensibly on the table.*)

WEBB   He's not fit for it, Padre.

PADRE I know what to do. There is provision made. It's
something I can do for him. (*Eating and drinking at the
appropriate words.*) The Body of our Lord Jesus Christ,
which was given for thee, and the Blood of our Lord
Jesus Christ, which was given for thee, preserve thy
body and soul into everlasting life.
Unto God's gracious mercy and protection we commit
thee.

(HARGREAVES *and* WEBB *move over to* HAMP *and gradually manipulate him until he is lying down in the straw.*)

HARGREAVES   All right, Corporal—you can leave him to us now.

CORPORAL   Sir. (*Exit.*)

WEBB   Have you finished, Padre?

PADRE Yes.

WEBB   Might as well be now, then.

(WEBB *moves* HAMP *gently until he is lying on his straw
bed, front downwards, with his face towards us.*)
I believe this is the surest place.
(*He cuts a small piece out of the backside of* HAMP's
trousers and gives him the shot of morphia.)
He won't know any more.
(*Puts two blankets over* HAMP.)

PADRE Thank you.

HARGREAVES   (*after a silence, and strangely*) Where's the soul, Padre?

PADRE It's here.

HARGREAVES   Is it? Are you sure?

PADRE Yes.

WEBB   How do you know?

PADRE I know. And so do you. If not, why are you concerned?

WEBB   There never was much of it, was there? Leave the guard
on duty. Come and get some sleep.

PADRE   No, I'm staying here.

WEBB   Why?

HARGREAVES   Tom—leave it alone.

WEBB   (insisting) Why?

PADRE   This is where my work is.

WEBB   I promise you he's out.

PADRE   Yes.

WEBB   So why not be practical? Remember we've all got to be on our best behaviour in the morning—C.O.'s ordered the smartest possible turn-out.

PADRE   Go and get some rest—please.

WEBB   There's nothing here. All that's here is a few hours of bloody nothing.

HARGREAVES   (looking back at HAMP, as they go out) He took it very well, you know.

WEBB   I suppose you were right about him. I suppose he was a likeable little bastard, wasn't he? God damn him and blast him.

CURTAIN

SCENE II

Next morning.
The scene is the same. Light: early dawn.
As the curtain rises, or perhaps even before, we hear the massive background sounds of the battalion approaching its assembly point for the ritual. Distant heavy gunfire. Nearer, marching feet, horses' hooves, cart wheels, etc., and cock crow.
Inside the barn, the CORPORAL and the GUARD are lifting HAMP, now strapped to a chair, preparing to take him out. WEBB is supervising, watched by HARGREAVES and the PADRE.

VOICE 1   (off) A Company—halt! Right turn! Order—hup!
                 (Drill sounds accordingly.)

VOICE 2   (off) B Company—halt! Right turn! Order—hup!

VOICE 1   (off) A Company—stand at—ease!
VOICE 2   (off) B Company—stand at—ease! No talking!
           (Drill sounds after each as appropriate.)
WEBB   (to HARGREAVES) Better get on parade, hadn't you, Bill?
HARGREAVES No—I'm not on this one.
WEBB   You'll be in trouble.
HARGREAVES C.O.'s permission. Unless you need me.
WEBB   No.
HARGREAVES Might as well start getting his letters written.
WEBB   (nodding to CORPORAL) All right, Corporal.
           (CORPORAL and GUARD carry HAMP out.)
           Have you seen to his kit?
HARGREAVES Yes. It's all here.
           (Indicating kitbag.)
WEBB   Thanks. I suppose they'll need you, Padre.
PADRE   Not yet.
WEBB   I'll let you know.
VOICE 3   (off) C Company—halt! Right turn! Order—hup!
VOICE 4   (off) D Company—halt! Right turn! Order—hup!
VOICE 3   (off) C Company—stand at—ease!
VOICE 4   (off) D Company! Now smarten up there! D Company,
           left—turn! Now let's have it properly this time! D
           Company, right turn! That's better! D Company—stand
           at—ease!
VOICE 3   (off) C Company—keep silence.
           (HARGREAVES has taken writing paper and pen, and has
           begun to write, obviously getting no further than the
           first few words.)
HARGREAVES (making conversation) All very untidy. The others
           weren't much better. Probably half asleep. (He notices
           that the PADRE has knelt down, preparing to pray.)
           Sorry.
VOICE 3   (off) A Company—stand properly at ease.
PADRE   Almighty God, we humbly commend the soul of this thy
           servant, our dear brother, into thy hands, most humbly
           beseeching thee that it may be precious in thy sight.
           Wash it, we pray thee, in the blood of that immaculate
           lamb that was slain to take away the sins of the world.
           (Meanwhile HARGREAVES has taken a whisky flask from

his pocket and drunk from it, and has realised that the
PADRE *has noticed.)*

HARGREAVES *(a little drunk, but the only sign is that it keeps him very*
calm) Might as well be honest.

PADRE Yes.

HARGREAVES No disrespect to the book of words. You could probably
do with some too. *(Offering flask.)* Did you have any for
the night?

PADRE No.

HARGREAVES I should have asked before we left you here.

PADRE I didn't think of it. *(He takes a drink.)*

HARGREAVES Medicine.

PADRE Thank you. *(He gives back flask.)*

HARGREAVES This makes a kind of ceremony of it too, you know.

PADRE Yes.

HARGREAVES Another way of marking the occasion. I haven't had
very much, by the way, if you're wondering. Enough to
get through the night. Tom and I—he kept on talking
about sleeping, but—of course, there's always the chance
that I'm more drunk than I know. He had more, but he's
probably using it up more quickly. Difficult to calculate
how drunk one wants to be. If I could think of somewhere else to go I'd get out of your way. All the same,
if you'll take my word for it, we're both marking the
occasion. Maybe the more ceremony the better. If we
surround it with words from your book and a few
toasts to old comrades and the full-dress ritual out there
we may not even notice it happening at all.

C.O. *(off)* Battalion! Battalion—shun!
(Massive drill movement in response.)

PADRE *(meanwhile in rapid prayer)* Almighty God, teach us
who survive, in this and other daily spectacles of
mortality, to see how frail and uncertain our own condition is——

C.O. *(off)* Slope—hup!
(Drill sounds again.)

PADRE O Saviour of the world, who by thy cross and precious
blood has redeemed us, save us and help us we humbly
beseech thee, O Lord.

WEBB   (off) Squad! Firing position—hup!

PADRE   Lord, have mercy on us.

WEBB   One round each man—take aim!

PADRE   Christ, have mercy on us.

WEBB   Fire!

(Sound of ragged firing, two ricochets, startled calls and wingbeats of rooks, frightened neighing from the horses, then silence. HARGREAVES *during this, having taken another swig from the flask, has gone out of the door to a position from which he can obviously see what is happening and is standing almost involuntarily in a formal 'attention' position.)*

PADRE   *(meanwhile)* O Lord God most holy, O Lord most mighty, O holy and most merciful Saviour, deliver him not into the bitter pains of eternal death. For that it has pleased thee to——

HARGREAVES   *(trying to be calm)* Not yet. It may not be finished yet. I don't think it is.

(Some crowd reaction, and shouts of 'Keep silence'.)

God knows it must have been atrociously bad shooting. Even worse than he expected.

(Sudden single shot, with sound reaction as before.)

PADRE   Oh my God—*no.*

HARGREAVES   *(walking back)* He was quite prepared to do it. Part of the job if there's any doubt. All part of the ritual.

PADRE   Almighty God, with whom the souls of the faithful after they are delivered from the burden of the flesh are in joy and felicity—for that it pleaseth thee——

*(*WEBB *appears in doorway, still unnoticed, putting revolver back in holster.* CORPORAL OF THE GUARD *behind him.)*

—to deliver this our brother out of the miseries of this sinful world—we give thee hearty thanks.

WEBB   Waiting for you, Padre. I'm told he's allowed a funeral.

PADRE   There will be no service yet, if that's what they expect.

WEBB   C.O. said he'd leave it to you to decide when.

(To CORPORAL.*)* Tell him no service now, Corporal.

CORPORAL   Sir! *(Exit.)*

WEBB   Means another parade, that's the trouble. Not much time before we move up again. Still, it's your job.

PADRE   I hope I shall do what I have to do at the right time. And I hope I shall not be ashamed of it.

WEBB   None of my business. But are you open to advice, Padre?

PADRE   I hope so, yes.

WEBB   Why not just let me finish the job now? Why not let us bury him and say no more about it? Too many bloody words, all along. Are you ready, Bill?

HARGREAVES   (*moving to go*) Yes. (*Then, looking back to* PADRE.) It's done now, why not leave it alone? It's a fact.

WEBB   I can vouch for that. And I'll tell you something else—I feel a hell of a lot better for it.

PADRE   (*shout*) No!

HARGREAVES   (*savagely*) Leave him alone. Leave us all alone to get on with our bloody war.

WEBB *and* HARGREAVES *go out.* PADRE *kneels in prayer, silently, with the sounds of the departing Battalion in the background.*

CURTAIN

PROPERTY LIST

ACT ONE

Inside Barn
- Straw
- Packing cases
- Eggs among straw
- Rope to bell outside (practical)

On one
- Paper
- Pen

} CORPORAL

PERSONAL
HARGREAVES
Notebook, pencil, cigarette-making equipment

HAMP
Mouth organ

GUARDS
Rifles

ACT TWO

Trestle table U.R.
Four chairs behind it
On it:
- Cloth
- Two carafes of water
- Four glasses
- Papers
- Notebooks
- Pencils
- Legal volumes
- Bible
- Each officer's cap

Packing cases D.R. and L.C. as desks and seats for HARGREAVES and MIDGLEY, and U.L. as seat for HAMP

On 'desks' of HARGREAVES *and* MIDGLEY
- Notes
- Legal volumes
- Caps